A Canoeing and Kayaking Guide
to the Streams of Florida

A Canoeing and Kayaking Guide to the Streams of Florida

Volume I, The North Central Panhandle and Peninsula

Elizabeth F. Carter
John L. Pearce

Menasha Ridge Press
Birmingham, Alabama

Copyright © 1985 by Elizabeth F. Carter and
    John L. Pearce
All rights reserved
Printed in the United States of America
Published by Menasha Ridge Press
First edition, fourth printing, 1990

ISBN 0–89732–033–6

Cover photograph of St. Mary's River by Butch Horn.
Cover design by Teresa Smith. Book design by Debbie Wong and
Barbara Williams.

Library of Congress Cataloging in Publication Data:

Carter, Elizabeth F., 1939–
    A canoeing and kayaking guide to the streams of
Florida.
    Includes index.
    Contents: v. 1. The North Central Panhandle and
Peninsula.
    1. Canoes and canoeing—Florida—Guide-books.
2. Rivers—Florida—Recreational use—Guide-books.
3. Florida—Description and travel—1981–   —Guide-
books. I. Pearce, John L., 1936–   . II. Title.
GV776.F6C37 1985   917.59   85-11596

Menasha Ridge Press
Route 3, Box 450
Hillsborough, North Carolina 27278

To our parents
  Amos and Virginia Fuller
  and Billee Pearce
For sharing their love
For the land and the rivers

Table of Contents

Introduction

The need for a comprehensive canoeing guide to Florida rivers became patently clear as the Florida Canoe Trail System, initially developed by the Florida Department of Natural Resources, faded more and more into oblivion. Established in 1971, the purpose of the Canoe Trail System was to identify and officially designate those waterways that possessed outstanding characteristics of interest to the canoeist, and to disseminate information about them to the public. By 1975, 35 rivers had been included in the system, and a small booklet, *Florida Canoe Trail Guide*, was provided free of charge.

Lack of funding in subsequent years reduced the information provided about the canoe trails to scanty data in a fold-out brochure. At present, the Department of Natural Resources can only send inquirers a photocopy of that brochure and a bibliography advising them of other sources of information.

This book, *A Canoeing and Kayaking Guide to the Streams of Florida: North Central Peninsula and Panhandle*, is the result of the authors' desire to fill the gap created by the downgrading of the Florida Canoe Trail program. We are greatly indebted to the personnel at the Florida Department of Natural Resources who have been helpful and supportive.

The information in this guide was obtained during three years of research and every mile of every waterway included was paddled by one or both of the authors. Our intention is to inform the reader about how to go about canoeing in north Florida. We will tell you how to get to the river and what to expect in terms of distance, difficulty, scenery, and anything else that you need to know to help you make a safe and enjoyable canoe trip.

Most of the waterways discussed in this guide can be paddled all year with normal rainfall. They will not be so isolated or specialized that they can be canoed only at certain times of the year when conditions are perfect. Neither have we included streams that are likely to be overpopulated with motorboats. Some of these rivers have access for motorized craft on their wider, clearer stretches, but on most of them another canoe or a small fishing boat is all that will be encountered. For that reason, we have not included information on north Florida's really large rivers—the Escambia, Apalachicola, and St. Johns.

Since this is a guide to rivers and streams, we have omitted inclusion of lakes, coastal estuaries, and bayous. There are thousands of them in north Florida and they have a special place in the canoeing world; unfortunately, time and space did not permit the extensive research that would have been needed to include them in this book.

For the adventurous, we will try to tell you where a river begins and what to expect if you choose to paddle above our first access point. For the curious, we will tell you what lies below the point where we chose to stop and why we stopped there. We will also mention some rivers and streams that you may cross on the highway that are not included in the book and tell you why not.

Any bookstore will yield a number of books that will give you detailed information about river safety, equipment, camping, and canoeing techniques. We will offer suggestions on these subjects when appropriate, but this book is a canoeing and kayaking guide and for the most part we will stick to that subject.

Almost day on the St. Marys River

Photograph by John Pearce

Friendly Advice

Without going into great detail, we would like to share some information with you based on our experiences camping and canoeing in north Florida.

Weather

North Florida is not tropical and has pronounced changes in the air and water temperatures. The high for the Tallahassee area in the summer is in the 90s and the low for most winters is in the 20s. Pensacola, Tallahassee, and Gainesville have comparable weather. It will usually be five to ten degrees warmer in the Ocala area.

Spring and fall are our most beautiful and comfortable seasons. We rarely have prolonged spells of cold weather until December and warm days have usually resumed by mid-March. It rains most during January and March and we will have an afternoon shower almost every day in July and August.

River water temperature can drop to the low 40s in the winter and, when combined with cold air, can result in hypothermia for a capsized canoeist. The same care should be observed when dressing for winter canoeing in north Florida that would be used in more northern climates. In the summer, exposure to the sun should be carefully monitored. Even cloudy and overcast days can produce enough ultraviolet light for severe sunburn to occur. Remember, too, that the reflection from sand and water can increase the danger of sunburn.

Insects

During the warm months, mosquitoes, sand gnats, and yellow flies can be a source of discomfort. Mosquitoes are usually confined to shady, wooded areas and are at their worst just at dusk and in the early morning. Most commercial insect repellents are effective in discouraging them. Yellow flies are usually present on hot, still days. They are rarely a problem after dark. They too are repelled by most commercial products, but it may take more of it and every piece of exposed skin must be covered. Sand gnats, or no-see-ums, are the reason that good tents have fine netting on the doors and windows. They are most common in marshy areas near the coast, but will occasionally be encountered inland. Insect repellent does not deter them, but application of something oily to the skin will. Some cosmetic bath oils or baby oil mixed with repellent is useful for this purpose.

Reptiles

There are several varieties of poisonous snakes in north Florida, but the chances are that you will rarely see one. Of the last 85 million visitors to Florida, only five were bitten by poisonous snakes and no one died. Use common sense when walking in the woods, never climb on or step over logs without checking for snakes, and avoid walking in palmetto palms or dense underbrush.

Alligators are another matter. If you are reasonably quiet, your chances of seeing alligators on most north Florida streams are excellent. Usually as soon as they see you they will slip into the water and swim away. If they do not, avoid approaching or annoying them in any way. In some more populated areas where the alligators have become accustomed to people, they are no longer shy and may be extremely dangerous.

Camping

Sandbars are the campsites of choice when they are available. They have fewer insects, no poison ivy, and they help to avoid the possibility of camping on private property. If no sandbar is available, look for a clearing in the woods on high ground. Camping in the swamp is definitely not acceptable. If possible, avoid camping at boat ramps or other access points. A quiet dirt road leading to the river may turn into the local party spot after dark.

Property Rights

A great deal of the land in north Florida is public land but there are often scattered parcels of private property even in the national forests. According to Florida law, public property extends to the mean high-water level. This is often difficult to determine, but the high-water marks on trees will give you some idea and sandbars are usually considered in the public domain. If confronted by a property owner, don't argue about it, just move on. It goes without saying that trespassing and posted signs should always be obeyed.

Roads

The price that we pay for remote, undeveloped, wilderness rivers in north Florida is the frequency of poor access roads. Many of our rivers are of the "delta-swamp" variety in which there will be a corridor of high ground on one or both banks, with a low, swampy area behind it. We also have an abundance of high, sandy ridges. As a result, most unpaved access roads to a river will suffer from deep sand pits in dry weather and wet bog holes during the rainy season. The authors have tried to give directions on paved roads as much as possible. This may result in a longer shuttle, but will probably be more reliable.

Leaving Cars Unattended

Some guidebooks will make suggestions about where you may safely leave cars. We prefer to let you use your own judgment. It is always best to arrange with someone to look after your car, and a small fee is worth the peace of mind.

Canoeing Skills

Don't assume that the canoeing skills you have developed elsewhere will qualify you for everything north Florida has to offer. Many of our streams are twisting, fast, and loaded with obstructions. They may also be miles from a road through sand hills or swamp. Four miles on a straight, spring-fed river is very different from four miles on a narrow, cascading stream with fifteen pull-overs. Read the trip descriptions carefully before you set out.

Geographic area covered in this volume.

Geology of North Florida

The state of Florida is a landmass which occupies a minor portion of the Floridian Plateau. This plateau is attached to the continental United States and is a partially submerged platform about 500 miles long and varies from 250 to 400 miles wide. It has existed for millions of years and is one of the most stable places on the crust of the earth.

Over the millennia, Florida has submerged and resurfaced from a series of ancient seas. The Coastal Lowlands are the most recent landmasses to have emerged from the sea. They are those areas that surround the hills of the highlands in the northern and western sections of the state and they make up the flatlands that are known as south Florida.

The Highlands of the north and west are geologically much older than the Coastal Lowlands and they reach their highest point at about 325 feet above sea level. Since the Florida peninsula is narrow, especially in the northwestern panhandle, it is often less than 50 miles from a high point of 300 feet above sea level to the Gulf of Mexico. The resulting gradient, combined with the terraces and ledges that have been left on the landscape with the recession of the seas, has produced the unique geological phenomena that have made north Florida rivers a paradise for canoeists.

The designation, *north* Florida, has no geographical boundaries. Geologically, it includes the Western Highlands, the Marianna Lowlands, the Tallahassee Hills, and the Central Highlands. In geographic terms, this includes an area beginning at the Perdido River west of Pensacola and continuing south to an imaginary line drawn from New Port Richey on the west to Orlando on the east. The rivers and streams that we have identified as north Florida waterways lie within this area.

Stream Description and Classification

The waterways described in this guide begin in the most northwestern part of the state and proceed east and south. Some north Florida streams are tributaries to larger rivers that constitute a drainage basin, but most are independent drainage areas themselves. A general description of the region and basin will be provided, followed by an overview of a canoe trip on the specific stream.

Information about access to the stream will always begin at a point that appears on the Florida Official Transportation Map, and will provide directions, to the nearest half mile, to readily identifiable landmarks.

The trip description will describe, in narrative form, each section of the stream including the distance between put-in and take-out, quantitative characteristics such as width, depth, and degree of difficulty, and the authors' evaluation of the scenery. The reader must bear in mind that rivers change, roads become impassable, land is fenced, and conditions alter on both land and water with flood or drought.

There are a number of classification systems by which the stream and the paddler can be rated as to the degree of difficulty and the amount of expertise required. Most of these systems are applicable to whitewater and are not particularly useful for north Florida waterways. Wilderness canoeing, of the type described in this book, is not without hazards and does require a repertoire of skills that do not lend themselves easily to a classification system. Sections of streams will therefore receive a general rating based on the terminology defined below and any specific skills needed will be discussed in the narrative.

Easy	Mostly smooth water with no significant obstructions. Paddling requires basic strokes, moderate skill, and endurance.
Moderate	Water with some current. Some obstructions possible such as cypress knees, pull-overs, or rocky shoals. Some sharp turns. Paddling requires fair skill in the draw and cross draw, some skill in reading moving water, the ability to effectively back paddle, and good endurance.

Strenuous   Fast water, many obstructions and/or pull-overs, sharp turns, narrow channels, possibly shoals or whitewater.
Paddling requires good skills in the draw and cross draw, the ability to utilize a high and low brace, some ability to ferry in current, good endurance, good skills in reading water, and good coordination with partner if paddling tandem.

Wacissa River
Photograph by Slim Ray

Springs of Florida

Springs are among the most beautiful and unique phenomena that the canoeist is privileged to see. There are over three hundred springs in Florida, more than any other state in the United States, and more than in any other country in the world. They are the natural outflow of water from the underground water system and vary from tiny rivulets trickling from the ground, to deep caverns far below the surface of crystal clear pools.

Most of Florida's springs are located along major rivers and are concentrated in the western part of north Florida. Some of the springs have been incorporated into state parks, national forest recreation areas, or privately owned tourist attractions. Many more of them remain hidden away in areas not yet touched by development. These secluded gems of blue and green and silver are the special reward for those who paddle a canoe.

When springs occur on the waterways described in this guide, every effort will be made to describe their location, appearance, and the name by which they are most commonly known. Springs do change; high water may obscure them and extreme dry weather may reduce their flow. Some have been purchased privately and are fenced from public access—even from navigable water. In many cases the land around a spring may be private property, but canoeists may enjoy the spring from their boat. It is usually unwise to camp beside a spring unless permission has been obtained from the landowner.

The springs named in this book are all listed in the State of Florida, Department of Natural Resources, Bureau of Geology Bulletin No. 31 (Revised), *Springs of Florida*. On the following page is a listing of the 27 major springs in Florida. Some springs flow into or are the source of a river or creek, i.e., Wakulla Springs are the source of the Wakulla River. Other springs occur, "in isolation", i.e., they break through the surface of the earth, create a pool, pond, or lake, and then seem to drain through underground waterways rather than on the surface.

First magnitude or major springs discharge water at an average rate exceeding 100 cubic feet per second.

Florida's 27 Major Springs

Spring Creek Springs	(Gulf of Mexico)
Crystal Springs	(Crystal River)
Silver Springs	(Oklawaha River)
Rainbow Springs	(Withlacoochee River-South)
Alapaha Rise	(Suwannee River)
St. Marks Spring	(St. Marks River)
Wakulla Springs	(Wakulla River)
Wacissa Springs	(Wacissa River)
Ichetucknee Springs	(Santa Fe River)
Holton Spring	(Suwannee River)
Blue Springs	(Chipola River)
Manatee Springs	(Suwannee River)
Weeki Wachee Spring	(Weeki Wachee River)
Kini Spring	(in isolation)
Homosassa Springs	(Homosassa River)
Troy Spring	(Suwannee River)
Riversink Spring	(in isolation)
Hornsby Spring	(Santa Fe River)
Blue Spring	(Withlacoochee River-South)
Gainer Springs	(Econfina Creek)
Falmouth Spring	(Suwannee River)
Chassahowitzka	(Chassahowitzka River)
Alexander Springs	(St. Johns River)
Blue Spring	(Withlacoochee River-North)
Silver Glenn Springs	(St. Johns River)
Natural Bridge Spring	(St. Marks River)
Fanning Spring	(Suwannee River)

Glossary of Terms

Put-in	Access point where canoes are put into the water to begin a canoe trip.
Take-out	Access point where canoes are removed from the water at the completion of a canoe trip.
Access	Point where a put-in or take-out may occur. A location on the river that can be reached by motor vehicle and where canoes can be off-loaded to the water.
Shuttle	The process of moving the vehicles from the put-in to the take-out and returning with the drivers in one car so that there will be transportation waiting at the end of the trip.
Pull-over	An obstruction in the water that requires getting out of the canoe and pulling it over—usually a downed tree.
Portage or Carry-around	Obstructions in the water that cannot be navigated or pulled over. The canoe must be taken out of the water and carried around.
Stob	A firmly ensconced stump, cypress knee, or snag that is partially concealed by the water.
S.R.	State Road
C.R.	County Road
F.R.	Forest Road
Blow-down	Trees that have loosened from their roots and have fallen across or into a river or stream frequently resulting in strainers.
Strainer	Debris (i.e., logs, trees, fence wire) in a waterway that permits water to flow through but may obstruct canoe, gear, or canoeist.

Scenery Rating

Beauty, being "in the eye of the beholder," is difficult to rate and is highly subjective. The following descriptions will be used, based on the authors' perceptions of most of the scenery for a given section of a waterway.

Superb   An outstanding example of undeveloped wilderness for that particular type of terrain. It should be clean, free of litter and/or signs of encroachment or should have some scenery of unique or unusual aesthetic value.

Excellent   A fine example of wilderness for that type of terrain with scenery of a consistently pleasing and rewarding nature.

Good   Clean, relatively free from litter and/or signs of development. Pleasant to canoe through.

Fair   Not unusually outstanding in any way. More litter than is acceptable, evidence of overuse or development.

Poor   Really flagrant misuse, overdevelopment, or littering. Disappointing and disturbing to a conservation-minded paddler.

Sweetwater/Juniper Creeks in the Blackwater Forest
Photograph by Elizabeth Carter

Rivers of the Western Panhandle

Perdido River

Photograph by John Pearce

Perdido River

The Perdido River originates in south Alabama with the confluence of Dyas Creek and Perdido Creek. It serves as the state line separating Alabama and Florida to the west, and is about fifteen miles from Pensacola. The Spanish name, which means *lost*, probably resulted from the hidden nature of Perdido Bay which is formed by the Perdido River before it reaches the Gulf of Mexico.

Except for the upper section near Dyas Creek, a very strenuous trip, the Perdido is considered an easy and relaxing canoeing river. It is located in a remote area and runs through deep forests with banks lined with juniper and cypress trees as well as other upland hardwoods. The stream alternates between straight sections with modest banks three to five feet high to long curves with generously-sized gravel and sandbars on the insides of almost every bend.

There are a number of small streams that drain into the Perdido; its major tributary is the River Styx that flows in from Alabama. The Alabama side of the river is primarily the property of private hunting clubs. On the Florida side, La Floresta Perdido Wildlife Management Area, a cooperative public hunting area managed by the Florida Game and Fresh Water Fish Commission, runs for many miles. Guns and dogs should not be taken on the river and the canoe camper should be careful to observe posted and no trespassing signs.

Because of the limited access and protected wildlife areas, the forests along the Perdido are heavily populated with deer and turkeys as well as wild hogs and bears. Local people also report an occasional sighting of a Florida panther along with the usual raccoons, opossums and beavers. The observant canoeist may also see otters and alligators and the fisherman may catch bream and catfish.

In periods of normal rainfall, the Perdido is a shallow river and the water will vary from being very clear to a tannish yellow color in areas where there is more siltation. There is no industrial development of any kind on its banks and very little agricultural activity. There are a number of excellent swimming holes as well as ample white sandbars for sunning and picnicking.

The upper part of the Perdido River, from Dyas Creek to the section called Three Runs is very remote and inaccessible. It is also almost unnavigable because of the many logjams and pull-overs that occur. These logjams are caused by the somewhat unusual characteristics of the red cedar tree which is abundant in this area. These trees have a multitude of closely spaced branches that break off to a stiletto sharpness. Furthermore, the juniper tree is easily blown over and with its shallow but widespread root system, both tree branches and tree roots become buried in the sandy banks on either side of the river. Since the red cedar is noted for its durability in contact with the soil, once down, they tend to stay there forever.

Below U.S. 90, the Perdido becomes tidal and begins to finger off into sloughs and bayous. It is frequented by large motorboats as well. Perdido Bay is a large body of water that is subject to waves and high winds and is not advisable for canoeing. The recommended canoe trail is from Three Runs to U.S. 90, a distance of about 34 miles.

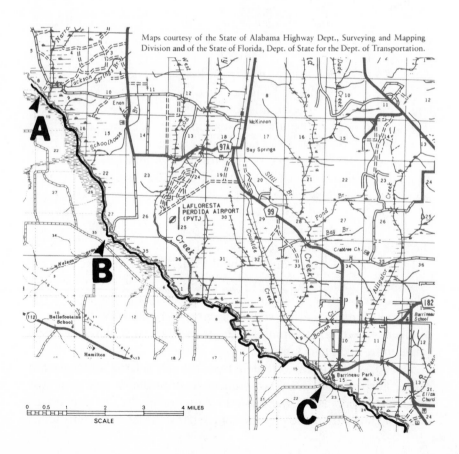

Maps courtesy of the State of Alabama Highway Dept., Surveying and Mapping Division and of the State of Florida, Dept. of State for the Dept. of Transportation.

Jackson Springs road to Old Water Ferry Landing (A–B): 5 miles

DIFFICULTY: Easy
SCENERY: Excellent
COUNTY: Escambia

ACCESS: From Pensacola, travel north on S.R. 29 to the junction with S.R. 182. Turn left (west) on S.R. 182 and proceed to S.R. 99. Turn right (north) on S.R. 99 and continue to the junction with S.R. 97A. Turn left (west) and continue for three miles until the paved road makes an abrupt turn to the right (north). Turn right, and travel for one and one-half miles to the first intersection with a graded road. Turn left (west) on this road and continue to the river.

TRIP DESCRIPTION: This is the most northern point recommended for a canoe trip on the Perdido. The river is 50 feet wide with heavily forested banks six to eight feet high. The water tends to be shallow and there may be some obstructions but it is an easy section and maneuvering is not difficult. There are large gravel bars on the insides of most of the curves. The forests on either side are hunting preserves, and it is a remote area with no public access. Schoolhouse Branch enters from the east about midway between Three Runs and Old Water Ferry Landing.

Old Water Ferry Landing to Barrineau Park (B–C): 10 miles

DIFFICULTY: Easy
SCENERY: Excellent
COUNTY: Escambia

ACCESS: Follow the directions for Section A–B to the point where S.R. 97A is reached. Turn left (west) on S.R. 97A and travel for three miles until the point where the paved road makes an abrupt turn to the right. Turn left (south) instead, onto a graded road. Follow this graded road to the river, a distance of about two miles.

TRIP DESCRIPTION: Greatly similar to Section A–B, the river continues to be remote, and varies between straight sections with clearly defined banks, to gentle curves. Several creeks including West Fork of Boggy Creek and McDavid Creek flow in from the east and the river becomes wider. The hunting preserves continue on both sides and there are frequent sandbars and gravel banks.

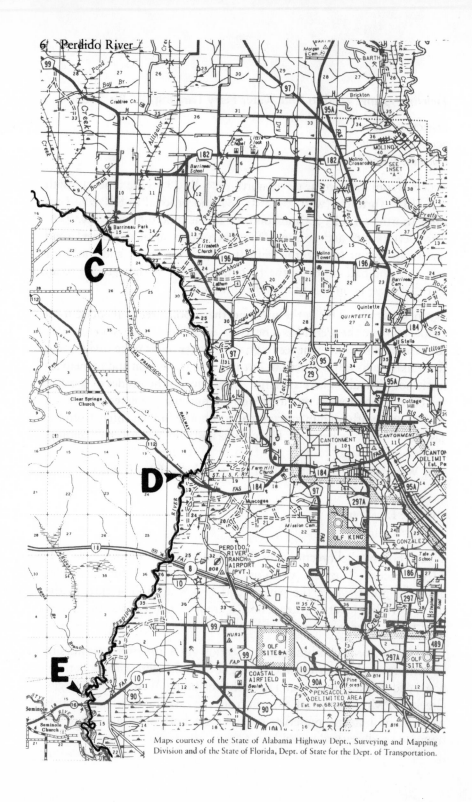

Maps courtesy of the State of Alabama Highway Dept., Surveying and Mapping
Division and of the State of Florida, Dept. of State for the Dept. of Transportation.

Barrineau Park to Muscogee Landing (C–D): 9 miles

DIFFICULTY: Easy
SCENERY: Excellent
COUNTY: Escambia

ACCESS: Follow the directions for Section A–B up to the point where S.R. 182 crosses S.R. 99. Turn left (south) on S.R. 99 and continue to the junction with S.R. 97. Turn right (west) onto the graded road and travel one-quarter mile to the bridge across the river. Access is on the northeast side of the bridge.

TRIP DESCRIPTION: The Perdido retains its shallow, winding character-istics with sandbars on the insides of turns alternating straight sections with deeper water. There is more frequent access to the river from the east side and this is a popular section for canoeing and fishing. There are a number of places where the presence of old pilings in the river indicates the location of former bridges. Just before reaching Muscogee Landing, there is an island in the river and a series of closely spaced pilings. The river narrows at this point and runs swiftly through the pilings giving a touch of excitement to the run.

Muscogee Landing to U.S. 90 (D–E): 10 miles

DIFFICULTY: Easy to Moderate
SCENERY: Excellent
COUNTY: Escambia

ACCESS: From Cantonment, travel west on S.R. 184 to the concrete bridge across the Perdido River. Access is on the northeast side of the bridge.

TRIP DESCRIPTION: There is a very large sandbar on the north side of the river at Muscogee Landing (S.R. 184) which is a popular swimming and sunbathing area for local people. This is the last of the campsite-sized sandbars, as the river becomes deeper and wider with either clearly defined banks, or swampy areas on either side. There are some sites that will provide space for two or three tents but they are scattered along this ten-mile section.

From Muscogee to Interstate 10 is just over two miles. Just below the south lane of the interstate is a drop where water rushes through a group of old stumps and pilings. If you have moderate maneuvering skills, stay to the middle right and follow the current. If you are unsure, scout from the left side and carry around if you choose.

An exception to the generally wider and deeper nature of the river occurs about one-half mile below the interstate highway. There is often a formidable logjam there as the river narrows and flows swiftly through the more confined area. An island divides the river just below this point and it is possible to paddle on either side. The island has a burned shed on the west side and appears to be used for camping.

Below the island, the river becomes much wider, the obstructions disappear, and the current slows considerably. Motorboat traffic increases with the advent of the deeper water and lack of obstructions. Hardwood forests line the banks with some swampy areas and small sloughs making an appearance.

TAKE-OUT (E): From Pensacola, travel due west on U.S. 90 for about 15 miles. There is no public access to the river from the bridge on U.S. 90, but there is a privately owned boat launch on the northeast side of the bridge. There is a fee for launching.

From U.S. 90 to Perdido Bay, the river continues to become wider, tidal and subject to wind. It is eight miles to Hurst Landing, the last public access before reaching Perdido Bay.

Streams in the Blackwater River State Forest

Some of the finest canoeing in north Florida can be found in the Blackwater River State Forest. The major waterway is the Blackwater River and its tributaries are Coldwater, Sweetwater, and Juniper creeks.

All of the Blackwater streams originate in south Alabama, and are characterized by being clear, shallow, and swift with a fine sand or gravel bottom. All have huge, sugar-white sandbars, and all are almost entirely free of encroachment. They are exceptionally fine streams for recreational canoeing because they are easy and fun to paddle as well as offering superb opportunities for camping, picnicking, and swimming.

There are ten designated campgrounds within the state forest, ranging from the fully equipped Blackwater River State Park to primitive areas with no facilities beyond picnic tables. Canoe campers can choose from a multitude of sandbars as well. The Andrew Jackson Red Ground Trail winds for 21 miles through the forest, tracing the earliest trade routes of the Indians and settlers in northwest Florida.

The red cedar is the predominant tree found near the streams with red maple, cypress, oak, and mixed hardwoods also common. Stands of planted longleaf pine are frequent on the higher ground. Fishermen occasionally catch black bass and small catfish from the streams, but the lack of aquatic vegetation greatly limits the fish population. A quiet canoeist may see raccoons, skunks, and opossums; perhaps even a turkey or deer, but the scarcity of fish leads to few sightings of turtles, otters, or wading birds.

Generally, the Blackwater Forest streams are only a few feet deep and are very clear and clean. There are no real springs in the area, but some of the tributaries flow into the streams with such clarity that they look like spring runs. The area just north of the forest is the Conecuh National Forest in Alabama, and as a result, there is virtually no development or agricultural activity to spoil the purity of the water.

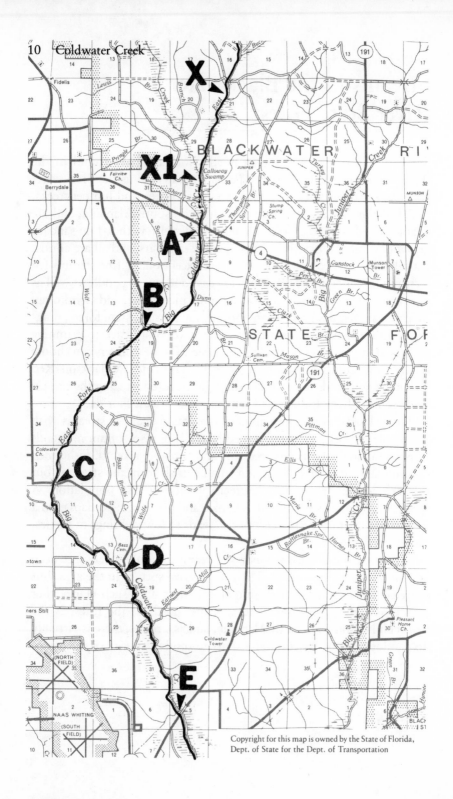

Coldwater Creek

Coldwater Creek is the most western of the streams in the Blackwater Forest and is said to be the swiftest. Flowing for some 20 miles through undeveloped land, it is very narrow in spots and has a gradient approaching three feet per mile. Obstructions include stobs, cypress knees, logs, and wide gravel bars that extend out into the stream from the sandbars. As a result of the swift water and the presence of obstructions, some maneuvering skill is needed to stay in the main channel. Lack of such skill leads to frequently running aground, an aggravating but harmless occurrence in the shallow water.

The upper section of the Coldwater, from Camp Lowry to S.R. 4 is not canoeable because the creek runs through an impassable swamp. However, it is possible to paddle from Camp Lowry down to Calloway Swamp and return; since it is a short and pleasant trip, a description will be included.

Camp Lowry to Calloway Swamp (X–X1): 4 miles round trip

DIFFICULTY: Easy
SCENERY: Excellent
COUNTIES: Santa Rosa

ACCESS: From the town of Munson, travel west on S.R. 4 for four miles to the intersection of a graded road, F.R. 13. Turn right (north) on that road and continue for four miles until it dead-ends into another graded road, F.R. 28. Turn left (west) on that road and continue for about one and one-half miles to a bridge across Coldwater Creek.

TRIP DESCRIPTION: Camp Lowry is situated on a shallow bend of very clear water with large sandbars. It is a primitive camping area with picnic tables being the only facilities provided.

Leaving the bridge, the stream is straight and lined with a variety of hardwood trees. Banks are four to seven feet high with only a few small sandbars becoming more swampy as you approach Calloway Swamp. Suddenly, the river channel ends abruptly in a monstrous logjam. The river is diverted to the west through a channel about three feet wide and some 75 feet long that flows into the swamp. It is possible to navigate a canoe through this channel, but difficult to pull it back through upon returning.

Calloway Swamp tends to be shallow with a white sand bottom, but there are some deep holes. It is thick with cypress, gum, and other wetland trees, as well as lily pads, colorful water weeds, and a variety of wild flowers. Overall, it is a beautiful spot.

It is possible to paddle around in the swamp but impossible to continue southward to where the river regroups above S.R. 4. Despite some areas that appear to be open in the southern area of the swamp the trees grow so close together that a canoe cannot pass between them.

State Road 4 to Jernigan Bridge (A–B): 4 miles

DIFFICULTY: Easy
SCENERY: Excellent
COUNTIES: Santa Rosa

ACCESS: From Munson, travel west on S.R. 4 for five miles to the bridge across Big Coldwater Creek. This will be the second bridge, the first having been the bridge across Juniper Creek.

Access is from a small dirt road on the northwest side of the bridge.

TRIP DESCRIPTION: This is a very beautiful and remote section of Coldwater Creek. The stream varies from 25 to 30 feet wide at the beginning to some 40 to 60 feet wide further down. The banks are up to eight feet high and some have colorful variations of pipe clay. There are some obstructions in the water, but they are not hazardous.

Jernigan bridge to Berrydale bridge (B–C): 5 miles

DIFFICULTY: Easy
SCENERY: Good
COUNTIES: Santa Rosa

ACCESS: From Munson, travel west on S.R. 4 to the bridge across Big Coldwater Creek. Continue on S.R. 4 for three miles west of the bridge to the junction with a paved road to the left (south), F.R. 1. Turn left and continue for about three and one-half miles to a wooden bridge. Access is on the southeast side of the bridge.

TRIP DESCRIPTION: The access is the site of the Coldwater Horse Stables and Field Trial Area. There is an improved campground with tables, running water, and restrooms. It is by reservation only, however. This is also the spot where most of the liveries start their canoe rentals and this section may be crowded from late May to early September.

As the creek flows downstream from the Jernigan bridge, it occasionally narrows to 25 to 30 feet wide and may be somewhat deeper in these spots. For the most part it is wide, shallow, and clear with many large sandbars. There are also two or three places where the stream runs over slight drops caused by cypress roots or rocks in the waterway. This adds a touch of spice to an otherwise leisurely trip.

Berrydale bridge to Tomahawk Landing (C–D): 4 miles

DIFFICULTY: Easy
SCENERY: Good
COUNTIES: Santa Rosa

ACCESS: From Munson, travel west on S.R. 4 to the bridge across Big Coldwater Creek. Continue on S.R. 4 for three and one-half miles to the intersection with a paved road. This is one-half mile west of the road to the Jernigan bridge. Turn left (south) on this road and continue for eight miles to the bridge across the Coldwater, the Berrydale bridge. The access is on the southeast side of the bridge.

TRIP DESCRIPTION: This is the section of the creek most heavily populated by tubers and on warm summer days may be congested. Fortunately, the confluence with the West Fork of the Coldwater occurs less than one mile downstream, resulting in a much wider waterway with room for all. The West Fork is canoeable from S.R. 87, a distance of just over one mile.

Shortly below the confluence of the two creeks is Party Island, a large, white sand island in the middle of the river. This is a favorite stopping place for picnicking and swimming. At the southernmost end of the island, the river branches, with the widest part flowing right, and a small stream flowing almost due left. This stream is a bypass that cuts off about one-quarter of a mile of paddling.

Tomahawk Landing to State Road 191 (D–E): 5 miles

DIFFICULTY: Easy
SCENERY: Good
COUNTIES: Santa Rosa

ACCESS: From Munson, travel west on S.R. 4 to the bridge across the Big Coldwater Creek. Continue on S.R. 4 for three and one-half miles to the intersection with a paved road. This is one-half mile west of the road to Jernigan bridge. Turn left (south) on this road and continue for about eight miles to the bridge across Big Coldwater Creek. After crossing this bridge, continue for about two miles to the road to Tomahawk Landing—it is clearly marked.

TRIP DESCRIPTION: Tomahawk Landing is a privately owned campground, launch area, canoe rental and outfitters' headquarters. Canoes and equipment may be rented and shuttles arranged for a fee. There is also a fee for launching private boats and for parking.

This section of the Coldwater has left the state forest and it is beginning to lose its remote nature. It is also wider and shallower and there are areas where saw grass grows along the banks as it becomes more influenced by saltwater.

TAKE-OUT (E): From Milton, travel north on S.R. 191 to the Coldwater Creek bridge. Below S.R. 191, Coldwater Creek continues for three more miles to its confluence with the Blackwater River. It is an additional ten miles down a broad, tidal river to the city of Milton.

Sweetwater and Juniper Creeks

Narrower and more twisting than Coldwater Creek, these two smaller tributaries of the Blackwater are usually canoed together, beginning on the Sweetwater.

It is possible to put in a canoe on Juniper Creek above S.R. 4, but it is an arduous trip and is not recommended. The stream is very narrow at that point, is canopied by trees, has high banks and many, many pull-overs. There is no access to Juniper Creek at the S.R. 4 bridge, but it is possible to put in at the S.R. 191 bridge and paddle the Juniper for less than two miles to its confluence with the Sweetwater.

Some canoeists prefer to start on the Sweetwater at S.R. 4. It too is narrow, has many obstructions, and is tedious except in high water. The best starting point is at the Munson School Road, a little over two miles downstream. The paddler still has the experience of the canopied stream for the two miles above the confluence with Juniper Creek without the ordeal of pulling over a number of logjams.

Because these are swift streams, some caution should be exercised. Do not paddle on the upper sections when the water is very high or flooded, watch carefully for logs and obstructions in the water and for overhanging trees. A moderate degree of skill and the ability to read moving water is helpful and will make a more enjoyable trip.

There is a primitive camping area at the bridge at Red Rock; picnic tables are the only facilities provided.

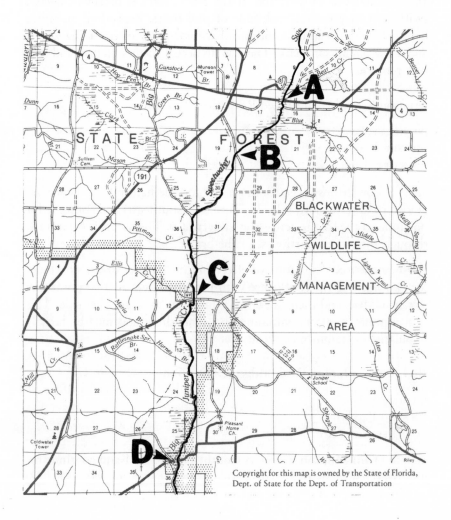

Copyright for this map is owned by the State of Florida, Dept. of State for the Dept. of Transportation

Sweetwater Creek at State Road 4 to Munson School Road (A–B): 2 miles

DIFFICULTY: Moderate
SCENERY: Superb
COUNTIES: Santa Rosa

ACCESS: From Munson, travel east on S.R. 4 just over one mile to the bridge across Sweetwater Creek. Access is 25 yards down a small dirt road.

TRIP DESCRIPTION: This section of the Sweetwater is narrow, shallow, swift, and may have a multitude of pull-overs, depending on water level. There is a beautiful canopy of hardwoods, clear, cascading water, and a few small sandbars. There is no access to this section and it is very remote.

Munson School road to Red Rock (B–C): 5 miles

DIFFICULTY: Easy
SCENERY: Excellent
COUNTIES: Santa Rosa

ACCESS: From Munson, go south on 191 for one-half mile to the second graded road to the left, F.R. 21. Turn left (southeast) and continue for one mile to the bridge across the Sweetwater. The access is off a track through the woods northwest of the bridge.

TRIP DESCRIPTION: The canopied effect and the narrow stream continues for two miles to the confluence with Juniper Creek. At that point, the stream widens and there are large, white sandbars on either side. This is a popular spot for swimming and sunbathing and may be heavily populated on summer weekends.

Red Rock to Indian Ford bridge (C–D): 6 miles

DIFFICULTY: Easy
SCENERY: Excellent
COUNTIES: Santa Rosa

ACCESS: From Munson, turn left (south) on S.R. 191 and continue for just over six miles to the first paved road that turns left, F.R. 72.

Turn left (east) and continue for three miles to the bridge across the Sweetwater-Juniper Creek. Access is on the northwest side of the bridge.

TRIP DESCRIPTION: The Red Rock picnic area is aptly named for the 40 foot tall sandstone bluff that occurs on the east bank just below the bridge. It is the most impressive of several red rock bluffs that are found on these streams. This clay can be used in making pottery and some of them have been turned into slides, adding another dimension to recreation on the river.

The stream continues to be wide and swift with very large sandbars on either side. Within a mile of the Indian Ford bridge, Alligator Creek flows in from the east bank. This is a shallow, canopied creek that can offer a shady spot for a last dip on a warm day.

TAKE-OUT (D): From Munson turn left on S.R. 191 (south) and continue for ten miles. Turn left (east) on a paved road, F.R. 86, and continue to the Indian Ford bridge. Access is on the northwest side of the bridge.

Blackwater River

The Blackwater River is said to be one of Florida's cleanest waterways. Like its tributaries, Coldwater, Sweetwater, and Juniper creeks, the Blackwater is characterized by swift, shallow water and beautiful sandbars. The color of its water is more tannic than those of neighboring streams, hence the name, Blackwater. This is somewhat of a misnomer since the water is actually a clear, slightly red color that is far from black. The Blackwater River has almost fifty miles of remote and undeveloped terrain making it an excellent choice for an extended canoe trip.

The red cedar continues to be the predominant tree along the banks of the Blackwater with other mixed hardwoods and wax myrtle as well. Longleaf pine, some planted by the forestry service, can be seen on the higher banks.

There are designated campsites at Blackwater River State Park, and primitive campsites may be found at Kennedy Bridge and Bryant Bridge.

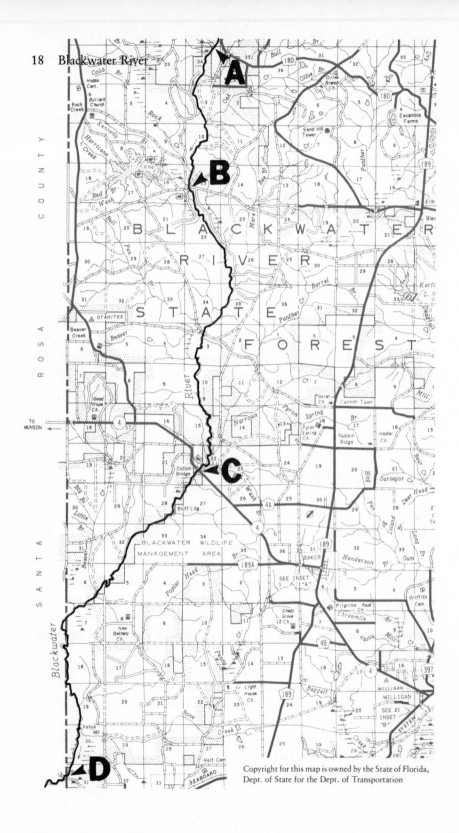

Alligator Branch (Chesser) Bridge to Kennedy Bridge (A–B): 5 miles

DIFFICULTY: Moderate
SCENERY: Excellent
COUNTY: Okaloosa

ACCESS: From Baker, travel north on S.R. 189 to the junction of S.R. 180. Turn left (west) on S.R. 180 and continue for about five miles. Just west of the point where this road becomes unpaved is a bridge across the Blackwater River.

TRIP DESCRIPTION: Similar to the uppermost sections of other rivers in this area, this section of the Blackwater is narrow, swift, and has many pull-overs. The banks are five to six feet high and heavily wooded with occasional small sandbars on bends in the stream. At low water this can be a strenuous trip but it is a remote and undeveloped area that is very attractive to the wilderness paddler.

Kennedy Bridge to State Road 4 (Cotton Bridge) (B–C): 10 miles

DIFFICULTY: Easy
SCENERY: Excellent
COUNTY: Okaloosa

ACCESS: From Baker, travel north on S.R. 189 to the junction of S.R. 180. Turn left (west) on S.R. 180 and continue for less than three miles to the point where a paved road, F.R. 24, turns left (south). Turn left and continue on this road for four miles to the bridge across the Blackwater. F.R. 24 is paved for only one mile beyond its junction with S.R. 180. Access is southeast of the bridge.

TRIP DESCRIPTION: This section is the beginning of the Florida Canoe Trail for the Blackwater River and is an easy and leisurely trip. It is primarily wide and shallow, with about a third of the distance being made up of narrow, deeper sections. There are numerous sandbars large enough to accommodate campers and there are few obstructions in the water. There is an established water gauge on Kennedy Bridge and a reading of around two feet is normal.

There is a wooden bridge, the Teaden Bridge, about halfway down this section. It is reached from S.R. 189 by turning onto F.R. 50 at Cannon Town. Below that bridge, the river has fewer of the deep, narrow sections and becomes generally wider and more shallow. It is still remote and wild.

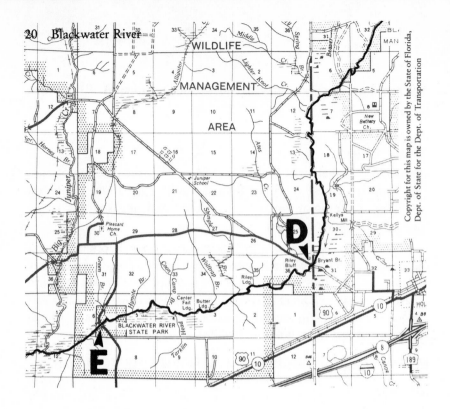

State Road 4 (Cotton Bridge) to Bryant Bridge (C–D): 12 miles

DIFFICULTY: Easy
SCENERY: Excellent
COUNTIES: Okaloosa, Santa Rosa

ACCESS: From Baker, travel west on S.R. 4 to the bridge across the Blackwater River. There is a park there with picnic tables and a boat ramp on the northwest side of the bridge.

TRIP DESCRIPTION: The river is very broad and shallow at this access and continues to widen as it flows toward Bryant Bridge. The banks vary from huge white sandbars to yellow clay banks from three to eight feet high. Below S.R. 4, the river occasionally flows through private property but for the most part maintains its wilderness character. There are a number of small creeks that flow into the Blackwater, and one of them, at Kellys Mill on Bone Creek, is sometimes used for an access. It is only two miles above Bryant Bridge and is difficult to find by road.

Bryant Bridge to Deaton Bridge (Blackwater River State Park) (D–E): 8 miles

DIFFICULTY: Easy
SCENERY: Good
COUNTIES: Okaloosa, Santa Rosa

ACCESS: From Holt, travel west on U.S. 90 for about one mile. Several graded forest roads turn right (north) off U.S. 90 with signs indicating that they lead to the Blackwater River Environmental Center. They all lead to F.R. 21 which leads to the wooden bridge across the Blackwater. Access is on the northeast side of the bridge. There is a primitive camping area at this spot.

Bryant Bridge is a popular picnicking and swimming spot as well as being a put-in and take-out site for canoe liveries. As a result, it may be congested on summer weekends.

TRIP DESCRIPTION: Shortly below the bridge, the river begins to turn to the west and it begins to change in character. Small streams flowing in create little sloughs that in turn feed into the river. These little sloughs become more common as the river nears the state park. Since this is a common day-use area, the river is overly littered and has lost its atmosphere of remoteness.

The Blackwater River State Park has a full range of facilities with the camping area being located about two hundred yards upstream from Deaton Bridge. Florida state parks close at sundown and those wishing to leave their cars inside will need to make arrangements with the ranger.

TAKE-OUT (E): From Holt, travel west on U.S. 90 to F.R. 23, turn right (north) on F.R. 23 which will be plainly marked as the route to Blackwater River State Park. Access is from the northwest side of Deaton Bridge.

Below the state park, the Blackwater continues to widen with more frequent sloughs that are now covered with saw grass. It is two miles to the confluence with Sweetwater-Juniper Creek and seven miles to the confluence with the Coldwater. It is 14 miles to the roadside park at the city of Milton. The broad, slow nature of the river and the advent of motorboat traffic usually discourages canoeists from proceeding below Deaton Bridge.

The Yellow River Basin

The Yellow River drains the highest point in Florida and is fed by nearly one hundred small streams and creeks as well as the Shoal River. It begins in south Alabama in the Conecuh National Forest and ends on the boundaries of the Eglin Air Force Base.

It is a swift flowing river that traverses a sparsely settled area, providing over fifty miles of wilderness canoe camping and touring. The Yellow is generally not as clear as the neighboring streams in the Blackwater Forest. The sand along the banks and the river bottom has more of a tan hue than white, resulting in the yellow appearance of the water. There is also more aquatic vegetation than in the rivers to the west so that fish are present, along with alligators, turtles, and water birds.

Other wildlife that might be seen include deer, turkeys, raccoons, and bobcats. Beavers are extremely active on this river and evidence of their handiwork is everywhere. A private hunting preserve shelters a large herd of Sika (Japanese deer) that may be glimpsed behind a high wire fence.

The trees along the river include river birch, willows, spruce pines, and many varieties of hardwoods. Lush vines, some with flowers, are frequently seen woven among the tree limbs.

With the confluence of the Shoal River, the Yellow turns almost due west and becomes much wider. It continues to flow for another 30 miles to Blackwater Bay but is broad and heavily used by motorboats and is of little interest to most canoeists.

The Yellow River

Alabama State Road 55 to Alabama State Road 4 (A–B): 13 miles

DIFFICULTY: Moderate
SCENERY: Excellent
COUNTY: Covington (AL)

ACCESS: From Florala, Alabama, travel northwest on S.R. 55 to Watkins Bridge which crosses the Yellow River. Access is from the northeast or northwest side of the bridge.

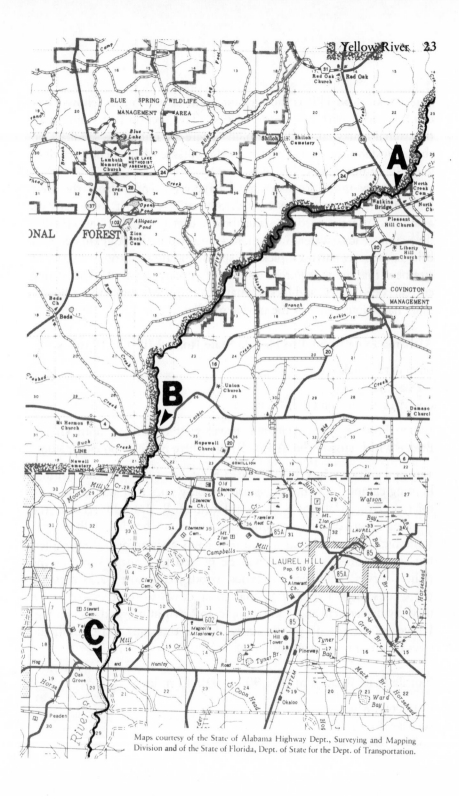

Maps courtesy of the State of Alabama Highway Dept., Surveying and Mapping Division and of the State of Florida, Dept. of State for the Dept. of Transportation.

TRIP DESCRIPTION: This is the furthest point at which the Yellow River can be canoed with any degree of ease. This section is winding with occasional banks up to 20 feet high. There are numerous sandbars on the curves and the deeper water on the outside of the bends provides good swimming holes.

About six miles downstream, a large creek enters from the west bank and the river widens considerably as a result. It soon narrows again and there is a rocky shoal below that point that can create a diversion at low water. Less than a mile from the Alabama S.R. 4 bridge, the river narrows, picks up speed, and flows through a series of strainers that may require a pull-over or carry-around. The strong current, deep water, and lack of maneuvering space make this a potentially hazardous spot for the novice paddler.

Alabama State Road 4 to Florida State Road 2 (B–C): 10 miles

DIFFICULTY: Moderate
SCENERY: Excellent
COUNTIES: Covington (AL), Okaloosa

ACCESS: From Florala, Alabama, travel west on S.R. 4 until Givens Bridge which crosses the Yellow River. There is access on either side.

TRIP DESCRIPTION: Just below the S.R. 4 access are several fishing-hunting camps; these buildings are the only ones that will be seen on the river from Alabama S.R. 55 to Florida S.R. 2. In this section, the winding nature of the river continues with many bends, sandbars, and some high banks. The strong current lends assistance to the paddler, but some maneuvering skill will be needed to manage some of the tighter curves. There are numerous woods roads (just tracks through the woods made by vehicles) that come down to the river; these are used by fishermen and local people for swimming and picnicking. However, there is no public access during this run, and overall, the river retains a remote atmosphere.

Florida State Road 2 to U.S. 90 (C–D): 17 miles

DIFFICULTY: Moderate
SCENERY: Excellent
COUNTY: Okaloosa

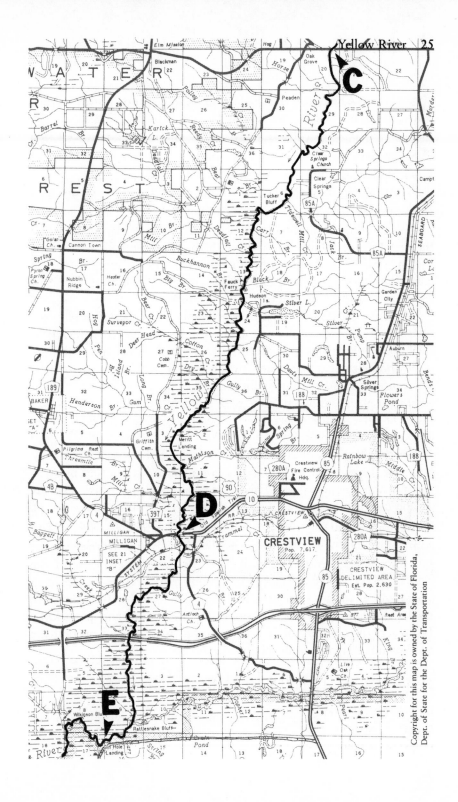

ACCESS: From Crestview, travel north on S.R. 85 to the junction with S.R. 2. Turn left (west) on S.R. 2 and continue to the bridge across the Yellow River. Access is from a paved boat ramp on the northeast side of the bridge.

TRIP DESCRIPTION: This is the beginning of the Florida Canoe Trail. The river becomes deeper and cloudier as it flows toward U.S. 90. The variation from steep banks to low sandbars with some swampy areas continues with the sandbars becoming smaller and less frequent during the first 15 miles. Bluffs up to 40 feet high are occasionally seen on the east side and may continue for one-quarter mile or more along the bank. There are myriad streams feeding the river from both sides and campsites are scarce until a few miles above U.S. 90.

Brightly colored markers on the trees indicate the placement of bush-hooks (baited lines attached to the lower limbs of trees to catch catfish; they can be dangerous to boaters who are unaware that there are fish-hooks hidden under the water on the ends of the lines). Boats with small motors may occasionally be encountered.

Silver Lake Landing, an improved access off a private road, occurs just over halfway down this section. There are several houses along the east bank at this point.

A very tall, yellow bluff marks that beginning of two miles of sturdy fence on the east bank. This is the boundary for a hunting preserve that protects a herd of Sika. This fence is rigorously patrolled. There is a good campsite across the river on the west bank opposite the end of the fence. About two miles above U.S. 90, the large sandbars resume, and there is ample camping space available on most of them.

U.S. 90 to Gin Hole Landing (D–E): 10 miles

DIFFICULTY: Moderate
SCENERY: Good
COUNTY: Okaloosa

ACCESS: From Milligan, travel east on U.S. 90 to the Yellow River bridge. Access is from a graded road that turns off U.S. 90 about one-quarter mile southwest of the bridge.

TRIP DESCRIPTION: The Yellow divides immediately south of the U.S. 90 bridge at a large island. At the southern end of the island is the Louisville and Nashville Railroad trestle that crosses the river. At one time the Yellow River was considered a navigable stream from Blackwater Bay up to this point which was called Barrows Ferry.

The sandbars decrease again below U.S. 90 as the riverbanks become much lower and more heavily wooded. Interstate 10 crosses the river about four miles below U.S. 90; there is no access. From Interstate 10, it is less than three miles to the confluence with the Shoal River. Just above this confluence, the Yellow River splits into several swift flowing runs and the Shoal, flowing in from the east, is not easily identifiable. After the Shoal joins the Yellow, it turns west and becomes much broader.

From this point on, the left (south) bank of the river is the property of Eglin Air Force Base and usage is restricted. Much of the property on the right bank is privately owned and posted. Groupings of houses and cabins occur on the north bank at regular intervals from this point to the take-out, but the roads that lead to them are not open to the public. With the advent of the deeper water and broader river, one encounters an increasing number of motorboats and the trip becomes less interesting. There are several access points on the south bank that are frequently used by the public at this time (1984). They are on the military reservation, however, and access may be closed in the future.

TAKE-OUT (E): From Crestview, travel south on S.R. 85 for four miles to the bridge across the Shoal River. Continue across the river for three-quarters of a mile to the first graded road turning right (west). Turn right, and continue for four and a half miles to a poorly maintained dirt track turning right. A sign, M.P. CAMP, CH 17, will be seen at that point. Turn right and follow this track for about half a mile to the river.

The Yellow River from Gin Hole Landing to S.R. 189 is easily accessible to motorboats and is not particularly desirable to the canoeist. For those wishing to canoe this section, it is nine miles long and the access can be reached as follows:

From Crestview, travel west on U.S. 90 to the junction with S.R. 189 at the town of Holt. Turn left (south) on S.R. 189 and continue for three miles to the river.

The Yellow River Delta, the 30-mile section from S.R. 189 to Blackwater Bay, is a maze of saw grass and tidal flats. It is often difficult to locate the main channel of the river. Blackwater Bay is a large body of water subject to high winds and waves.

The Shoal River

The Shoal River is the major tributary of the Yellow River and, like the Yellow, drains out of some of the highest land in Florida. It flows west for the first fifteen miles, then turns southwest and almost parallels the Yellow for seven miles until the confluence with Titi Creek. At that point, it flows west again until its confluence with the Yellow just above Rattlesnake Bluff.

The Shoal is a swift, sandy waterway with tan colored water that is seldom more than a few feet deep. It is narrow and twisting and, except for an occasional logging bridge or isolated county road, is a fine example of north Florida wilderness. Campsites are not plentiful, but there are occasional sandbars that are large enough to accommodate a small group.

State Road 285 to State Road 393 (A–B): 10 miles

DIFFICULTY: Moderate
SCENERY: Excellent
COUNTIES: Walton, Okaloosa

ACCESS: From De Funiak Springs, travel west on U.S. 90 to the junction with S.R. 285. Turn right (north) and continue for about three miles to the bridge across the Shoal River. Access is poor from the northwest side of the bridge. There is a sandy trail southwest of the bridge that leads to a good access but the road itself is questionable. It should be checked before use by on-road vehicles.

TRIP DESCRIPTION: This section of the Shoal is narrow, shallow, and characterized by high sandbanks, some sandbars, and many twists and turns. There are over a dozen small streams and rivulets that feed into the river, most of them clean and shallow, but some make little sloughs that are covered with greenery. About four miles downstream, the Crowder Cemetery Road crosses the river via a wooden bridge. The river is narrow at this point with steep banks and there is usually a logjam against the pilings under the bridge. At the high-water levels this situation can be hazardous and it should be approached with caution. There is a similar situation two miles downstream at the Pond Creek road bridge. The banks are lower but there is often debris caught up under this bridge as well.

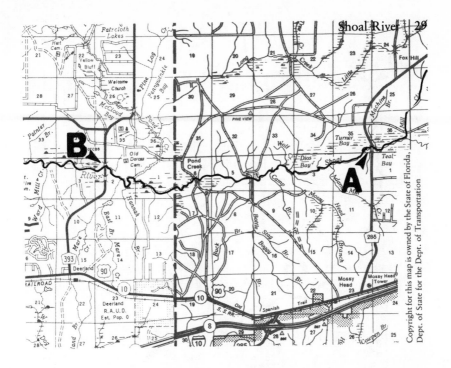

After passing under this bridge it is two miles to the confluence of Pond Creek. This is a wide creek as large as the Shoal at their junction. The river becomes broader below this point and it is only one mile to the access at S.R. 393.

State Road 393 to U.S. 90 (B–C): 8 miles

DIFFICULTY: Easy
SCENERY: Excellent
COUNTY: Okaloosa

ACCESS: From Crestview, travel east on U.S. 90 seven miles to the junction with S.R. 393. Turn left (north) and continue for three miles to the Shoal River. Access is on the southwest side of the bridge.

TRIP DESCRIPTION: Myriad small streams continue to feed into the Shoal keeping the current lively. It is broader and there are several good campsites on sandbars. The bends are gentler and there are some straight sections as well. Three miles below S.R. 393 is a two-mile-long section that ends in a bend to the south. The river then continues south to U.S. 90.

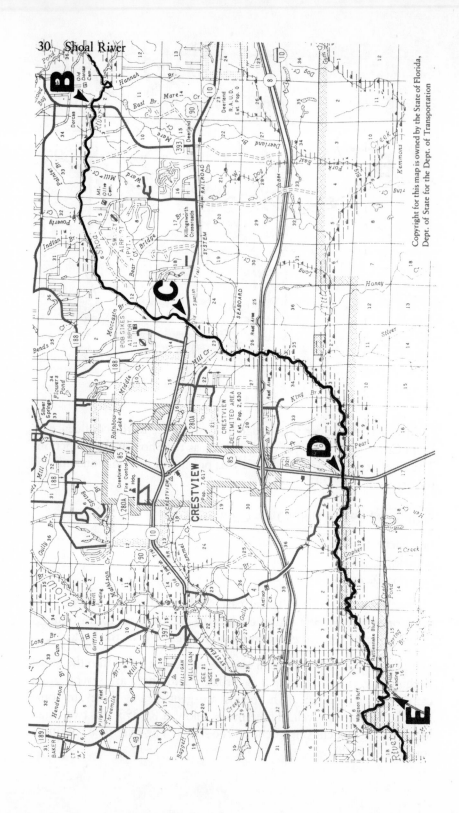

U.S. 90 to State Road 85 (C–D): 10 miles

DIFFICULTY: Easy
SCENERY: Excellent
COUNTY: Okaloosa

ACCESS: From Crestview travel east on U.S. 90 three miles to the bridge over the Shoal. Access is on the southeast side of the bridge at a concrete ramp.

TRIP DESCRIPTION: The river has widened to about one hundred feet with higher, heavily wooded banks. There are still sandbars on the insides of bends that are adequate for campsites, but most of the property on both sides is posted. Less than three miles downstream the river passes under Interstate 10 with no access. Below the interstate the river begins to change. The banks lower to one to four feet high and are lined with lowland hardwoods and spruce pine.

About three miles below the interstate, Titi Creek enters from the left bank. The mouth of this creek is 35 feet wide and surprisingly, the Shoal narrows at this point to 50 to 75 feet wide and flows very swiftly for 100 yards before widening out again. Some sandbars are evident below Titi Creek and small ponds begin to appear on the outside of some of the curves. Reeds and lily pads become evident; small fishing boats may be encountered in these quiet pools. The river begins to lose some of its remoteness as there are a number of places accessible by vehicles.

State Road 85 to Gin Hole Landing (D–E): 8 miles

DIFFICULTY: Easy
SCENERY: Good
COUNTY: Okaloosa

ACCESS: From Crestview, drive south on S.R. 85 to the Shoal River bridge. Access is on the northeast side of the bridge at a wayside park.

TRIP DESCRIPTION: Below this access the banks become lower again and in some places actual swamps appear on both sides of the river. The river alternately narrows and widens until just above its confluence with the Yellow where it becomes very narrow for nearly a mile. Campsites are scarce on this section. The best choice is on a bluff four miles below S.R. 85 on the left bank. Below the bluff private camps begin to appear and some of them are eyesores with old cars and appliances having been thrown over the banks.

In this area the river begins to break into runs and narrows and in some places is completely canopied. Sharp turns and obstructions in the river are encountered. The confluence with the Yellow River is undramatic since just above the Shoal, the Yellow has also broken up into separate runs and narrows. The junction is clearly defined, however. Gin Hole Landing is about one-half mile downstream from the confluence of the rivers on the south bank on the property of Eglin Air Force Base. It is not posted and is in common usage by the public at this time (1984).

TAKE-OUT (E): From Crestview, travel south on S.R. 85 for four miles to the bridge across the Shoal River. Continue across the river for three-quarters of a mile to the first graded road turning right (west). Turn right, and continue for four and a half miles to a poorly maintained dirt track turning right. A sign, M.P. CAMP, CH 17, will be seen at that point. Turn right and follow this track for about half a mile to the river.

The Yellow River from Gin Hole Landing to S.R. 189 is easily accessible to motorboats and is not particularly desirable to the canoeist. For those wishing to canoe this section, it is nine miles long and the access can be reached as follows:

From Crestview, travel west on U.S. 90 to the junction with S.R. 189 at the town of Holt. Turn left (south) on S.R. 189 and continue for three miles to the river.

The Yellow River Delta, the 30-mile section from S.R. 189 to Blackwater Bay, is a maze of saw grass and tidal flats. It is often difficult to locate the main channel of the river. Blackwater Bay is a large body of water subject to high winds and waves.

Choctawhatchee River

The Choctawhatchee River is over 170 miles long from its headwaters in Barbour County, Alabama, to the Choctawhatchee Bay near Fort Walton Beach, Florida. Of this length, there are over 100 miles of excellent canoeing, making it one of the finest touring rivers in northwest Florida. Not only is it a scenic river of high ecological significance, it is also very remote, limited in access, and offers an unusual opportunity for an extended wilderness experience.

The Choctawhatchee is a broad, shallow river that is usually yellow in color. It has an annual flooding pattern that is primarily responsible for the lack of development along its banks. The upper sections are characterized by high limestone banks, rocky shoals and drops, and sections of cascading water. After entering Florida, the river is calmer but more remote and has huge sandbars. The terrain varies from floodplain forests with upland hardwoods and pine hammocks to marshes and swampy wetlands. Wildlife is plentiful and a wide variety of animals indigenous to north Florida may be sighted along the banks. Beavers, in particular, have made an astounding comeback on the Choctawhatchee.

Major tributaries of the Choctawhatchee in Alabama include Judy Creek, the East Fork of the Choctawhatchee, the Little Choctawhatchee, and the Pea River. In Florida, Wright Creek, Holmes Creek, and several springs including Blue Spring and Morrison Spring feed the river.

Dale County Road 36 to Alabama State Road 27 (A–B): 6 miles

DIFFICULTY: Moderate
SCENERY: Good
COUNTY: Dale (AL)

ACCESS: From Midland City, Alabama, travel north on C.R. 59 to the intersection with C.R. 36. Turn left (west) and continue for one-half mile to the West Fork of the Choctawhatchee. Access is on the southwest side of the bridge.

TRIP DESCRIPTION: At the put-in on C.R. 36, the river is about 35 feet wide, shallow, and has a moderate current. It soon widens to 50 feet and at normal or slightly less than normal water there are a series of rocky shoals that stretch across the entire width of the stream. These

33

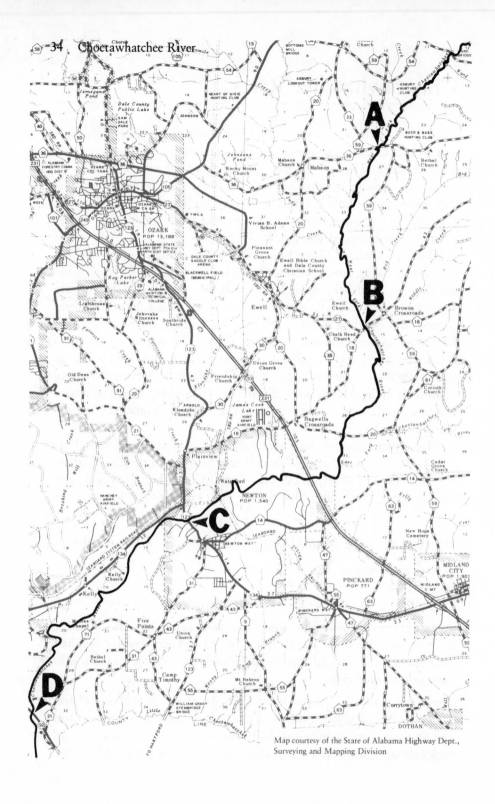

Map courtesy of the State of Alabama Highway Dept.,
Surveying and Mapping Division

shoals will require some skill in maneuvering to keep from running aground. The river is a drop-and-pool waterway with the short pools having a modest current followed by a stretch of faster water over the shoals.

Judy Creek enters the river about three and one-half miles downstream. This creek is an alternate access to the Choctawhatchee at normal to high water and has several interesting drops in its two-mile run from C.R. 36 to its confluence with the river.

Below Judy Creek, the river bottom becomes sandier and shallow, but there are still shoals across the river. Just above S.R. 27, there is a two-foot drop over a rocky ledge that may be troublesome to the novice paddler. It should be run on the extreme left and may be portaged if necessary. It is two and one-half miles from Judy Creek to S.R. 27.

Alabama State Road 27 to State Road 123 (Newton, Alabama) (B–C): 8 miles

DIFFICULTY: Moderate
SCENERY: Good
COUNTY: Dale (AL)

ACCESS: From Midland City, Alabama, travel north on C.R. 59 to the intersection with C.R. 27. Turn left (west) on C.R. 27 and continue to the bridge across the West Fork of the Choctawhatchee. A poor access is on the southwest side of the bridge.

TRIP DESCRIPTION: The shoals increase below the S.R. 27 bridge, and are frequently in sight of each other down to the confluence with the East Fork of the Choctawhatchee. The bridge from Bagwells Crossroads crosses the river about three miles down from the put-in, but there is no access. It is another mile to the confluence with the East Fork. There is a strong current at that point, and the river widens to 100 feet.

The drop and pool characteristic ends and the river proceeds with a constant current. There are a few small shoals below this point and a few houses begin to appear. The banks are 10 to 15 feet high with an occasional sandbank where livestock come down to the water. It is one mile from the confluence of the East Fork to U.S. 231. This is a dual lane bridge and access from this road would be very difficult.

Just below U.S. 231, on the south bank, a stream has cut a deep crevasse in the limestone as it enters the river. It is possible to paddle into this opening for a short distance and to look overhead at a beautiful fern fall.

One mile further downstream, a large sandbar occurs on the south bank. This bar used to be an island; it is the result of a change of direction in the flow of the river. It is an excellent campsite for a large party of campers. A very pretty stream flows into the river at the east end of this site that is worth a short walk to see.

About one and one-half miles further downstream a railroad trestle crosses the river. Just downstream of it is a large sandbank on the northwest side that is heavily used as an access point.

It is another mile and one-half to the S.R. 123 bridge; access to the river is very poor here. A canoe livery just above the bridge offers canoe rentals, shuttle service, and camping and launching facilities for a fee.

Alabama State Road 123 to State Road 92 (C–D): 8 miles

DIFFICULTY: Easy
SCENERY: Good
COUNTY: Dale (AL)

ACCESS: From Midland City, Alabama, travel north on S.R. 134 to the town of Newton. At this point, S.R. 123 will have joined S.R. 134. Continue north until crossing the Choctawhatchee River. Access from the canoe livery is reached via Waterford road, the first graded road to the right after crossing the bridge. Access from S.R. 123 is on the northwest side of the bridge; it is a poor access.

TRIP DESCRIPTION: Just below the S.R. 123 bridge are the pilings from an old mill that can be troublesome depending on the water level. Approach with caution and watch for debris that may have been caught, creating a strainer. There is usually a clear passage on the northwest side.

This section is a pleasant trip with high vertical banks and a good current. Little maneuvering skill is needed after passing the site of the old mill. Because of the high banks, campsites are scarce. There are two points where modest sandbanks line the river and a small party could camp but they might have to share facilities with livestock from nearby pastures.

Alabama State Road 92 to State Road 167 (D–E): 9 miles

DIFFICULTY: Easy
SCENERY: Good
COUNTIES: Dale (AL), Geneva (AL)

ACCESS: From Midland City, Alabama, travel north on S.R. 134 to the town of Newton. Just before reaching Newton, S.R. 123 will merge from the left (west). Turn left (west) on S.R. 123 and continue for about eight miles until it intersects with S.R. 92. Turn right (north) on S.R. 92 and continue to the bridge across the Choctawhatchee River. Access is on the west side of the bridge on either side of the road.

There is a canoe livery about one-quarter mile west of the bridge where canoe rentals and shuttle service may be arranged.

TRIP DESCRIPTION: There is a nice sandbar at the put-in that is popular with swimmers and sunbathers on warm weekends. In the next three miles to U.S. 84, the banks are sloping and heavily wooded. A possible campsite is at the point where the Little Choctawhatchee enters the river about one and one-half miles downstream from U.S. 92.

At U.S. 84 is an access to the river from a boat ramp on the southwest side of the bridge. Construction is underway here for a new bridge, so this access may change (1984). There is another large, popular sandbar at this access and for the next two miles there are numerous spacious and high sandbanks that are suitable for camping. The confluence with Pates Creek introduces sloping heavily wooded banks again and an end to the sandbars.

Three miles further downstream Claybank Creek enters from the northwest. Just up this creek, and in sight of the river, is a large sandbar that would provide camping space for several tents. About one mile below Claybank Creek the bridge at S.R. 167 is reached.

Alabama State Road 167 to Geneva, Alabama (E–F): 12 miles

DIFFICULTY: Easy
SCENERY: Good
COUNTY: Geneva (AL)

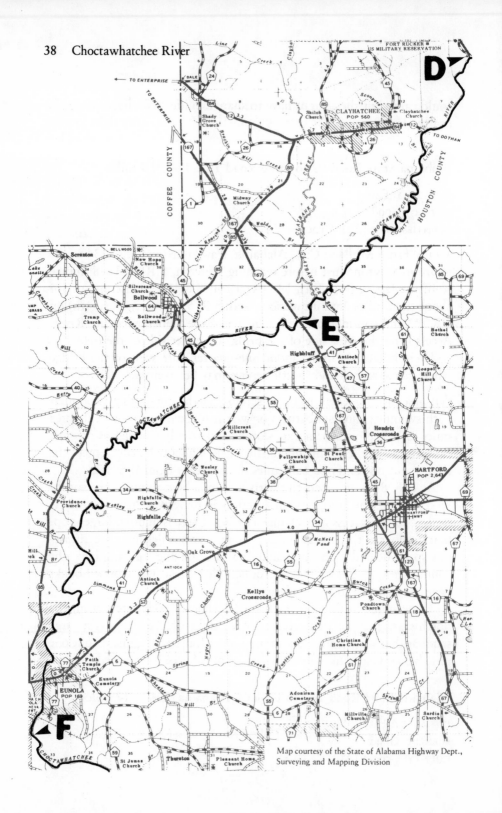

Map courtesy of the State of Alabama Highway Dept.,
Surveying and Mapping Division

ACCESS: From Dothan, Alabama, travel west on S.R. 52 through the town of Hartford to the intersection with S.R. 167. Turn right (north) on S.R. 167 and continue to the bridge across the Choctawhatchee River. Access is on the southwest side of the bridge.

TRIP DESCRIPTION: The banks of the river become higher at S.R. 167; shortly below this access, there is a high, wooded bluff on the southeast side that follows the river for about one-quarter mile. It becomes lower as the river bends to the left revealing a large sandbar, suitable for camping, on the left bank. This is the only good campsite for the next two miles as the banks continue to be high down to Bellwood Bridge. There is no access to the river at Bellwood Bridge.

Shortly below this bridge, the river begins a long loop to the west. There are three small streams that cut across this loop that are not navigable at present (1984). Several years of annual flooding could result in a change in the riverbed and this loop may be gone.

At the end of the loop is a large sandbar on the north bank with an almost vertical bank on the south side. Although there are several more sandbars in the following miles, they are very low and a rise in water level would make them doubtful campsites. It is over six miles to the next good campsite.

Interspersed with these low sandbars are vertical banks and the entrance of Bames Creek. Very large alligators have been observed in this section.

About six miles downstream from the put-in, there is a bend to the east in the river and the relics of two old docks can be seen on the east bank. There are some low pastures on the right bank that could be used for camping with permission from the owners but would probably have to be shared with livestock.

As the river turns south, the banks become very high with pastures on top. A rock bluff will be observed on the west bank and is followed one-half mile downstream by a boat ramp on the east bank. The access to the ramp is from Highfalls, a small community located on Geneva C.R. 41.

Shortly below this access, there are several large sandbars suitable for camping. These bars have access from a road, however, and may be used for swimming and sunbathing. Downstream from these sandbars is another high, well-wooded bluff on the west bank. There is also a beaver dam on the east side with a lake behind it.

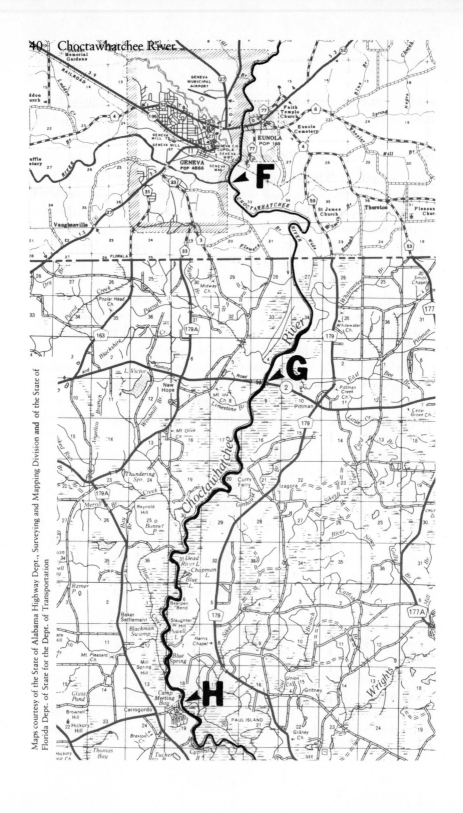

As the river bends to the east, sheer rock walls, 15 feet high, begin to appear with beautiful fern falls dripping down. This type of terrain continues almost to S.R. 52. One-half mile downstream from S.R. 52 there is an old railroad bridge that swings on the center piling. This indicates that it was probably built in the early 1900s when steamboats still used the river. The pilings for the bridge are made of brick and the center piling has an unusual wooden structure built around it to protect it from floating trees during floods. There is a boat ramp at the park at river junction about one-half mile below this bridge.

Geneva, Alabama, to Florida State Road 2 (F–G): 8 miles

DIFFICULTY: Easy
SCENERY: Good
COUNTIES: Geneva (AL), Holmes

ACCESS: There is a boat ramp in the park located at the point where the Pea and Choctawhatchee rivers join, just south of Geneva. Turn west at the red light and then south on the first paved street to the left (one block). Continue for three blocks, cross the railroad tracks, and turn left on the first paved street. Continue for about one and one-half miles to the park and boat ramp.

TRIP DESCRIPTION: Just below the park Pea River joins with the Choctawhatchee. A sizable river itself, the Pea flows through south Alabama to the north of and almost parallel to the Choctawhatchee. It is a beautiful canoeing river and is excellent for canoe touring.

After the confluence with the Pea, the Choctawhatchee widens to some 300 feet and remains wide over the next few miles, gradually narrowing to its customary 150-foot width. The banks continue to be high and heavily wooded, with large sandbars in the curves. It is about five miles from the put-in at S.R. 52 to the Florida state line. Somewhere in the area of the state line there is a clay bank 20 feet high on the east side with a large field on top. From this clay bank it is about four miles to Florida S.R. 2.

Florida State Road 2 to Camp Meeting Bay (G–H): 11 miles

DIFFICULTY: Easy
SCENERY: Good
COUNTY: Holmes

ACCESS: From Bonifay, travel west on U.S. 90 to the intersection with S.R. 177A, turn right (north) on S.R. 177A, and continue to the intersection with S.R. 2. Turn left (west) and continue for four and one-half miles to the bridge across the Choctawhatchee. There is not an adequate access at this bridge, but there are accesses used by local fishermen on the east side of the bridge, both to the north and to the south. These are rough tracks that run beside the river for one-half mile in either direction.

TRIP DESCRIPTION: For the next ten miles, the river is broad, shallow, has a good current, and some of the largest sandbars found on any north Florida waterway. Sandbars of 10 to 15 acres in size are not uncommon. These sandbars are frequently covered with tracks of the various birds and animals that inhabit this area. Of particular interest is the evidence of the beaver population. Practically driven to extinction by trappers in the early part of the century, they are obviously alive and well on the Choctawhatchee! The overnight camper on one of these large sandbars will often have a unique opportunity to see or hear beavers going about their business of dragging willow branches to the water, feeding, stripping the bark of river birch, or slapping their tails on the water.

This section of the river is very remote and it is unusual to see another boat. The few boats encountered will be small fishing boats many of which do not carry motors but are propelled by sculling.

There is a concrete landing at Curry Ferry, about two miles downstream from S.R. 2 on the east bank, and another landing on the west side at the end of a graded road opposite Dead River Lake, three more miles downstream.

Some five miles below this last landing is Cork Island. This is only an island at high water, since at low water the east channel is blocked by sand. On the west bank, just opposite the island, is Blue Spring. This is the most northwest spring in Florida and is accessible only by boat. It is a deep, clear blue hole suitable for swimming. Considering its remoteness and the swampy, inaccessible area around it, this water is probably safe for drinking if needed. Just over one mile below Blue Spring is Camp Meeting Bay.

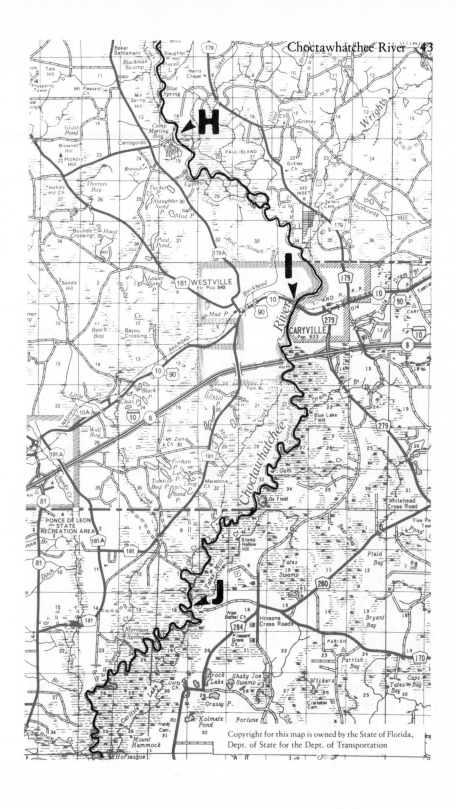

Camp Meeting Bay to U.S. 90 (H–I): 6 miles

DIFFICULTY: Easy
SCENERY: Good
COUNTY: Holmes

ACCESS: From Westville, travel north on S.R. 179A for three miles to an intersection where the road on the left (west) will be paved and the road on the right (east) will be graded. Turn right (east) on the graded road and continue for one mile to the river. Access is from a concrete ramp.

TRIP DESCRIPTION: Camp Meeting Bay is a small community of cottages located on the top of a high, sandy bluff. Despite the height, most of the houses are built on pilings.

Three miles downstream from this put-in is the site of a former island. Annual flooding has washed away all but its northern tip and the channel that went around it to the east now has trees growing in it. The channel to the west may also be obstructed with trees, but is navigable.

One mile below this point, is Wrights Creek Landing on the east bank. The landing is about one-half mile above the confluence of Wrights Creek and is reached from S.R. 179. There is a small settlement of houses there. With the confluence of Wrights Creek, the river widens noticeably, the sandbars cease, and the current slows—this is less than two miles above U.S. 90.

U.S. 90 to Hinsons Cross Roads (I–J): 12 miles

DIFFICULTY: Easy
SCENERY: Good
COUNTIES: Washington, Holmes

ACCESS: From Caryville, travel west on U.S. 90 for less than one mile to the river. Access is from a concrete boat ramp on the southeast side of the bridge.

TRIP DESCRIPTION: At U.S. 90, the Choctawhatchee is about one hundred yards wide, shallow, and has little current. This continues for two miles; in this section are the last of the large sandbars suitable for camping.

Interstate 10 crosses the river one mile below U.S. 90. There is no access to the interstate from the river. About one mile below the interstate highway is an island whose west passage is blocked by trees. The east passage is partially obstructed with the debris caught up by old pilings. A large sand strip leads off to the east and evidently is a part of the river when the water is high. This is the last sandbar. Just below this point, the river narrows to 50 yards and the current picks up. The banks are low, but very heavily wooded. Willows and river birch often hang off the banks into the waterway and occasionally the banks are very swampy.

Five miles downstream from U.S. 90 is a rapid at Gum Creek. The main river flows to the right—a portion flows off to the left, over a drop, through an obstructed area, and rejoins the river on the other side of a small island. The fast water can be heard as it is approached, but scouting is difficult. Even though the run is only 15 yards long, it has a standing wave and a crosscurrent as well as the complication of downed trees. If in doubt, follow the main channel to the right.

In this area, the river begins to make wide oxbow bends that create islands. On one of these bends to the west are red reflectors nailed to the trees that indicate an access at Old Creek. This access is reached from S.R. 181 out of Westville and cannot be seen from the river.

Shortly below this point, there is another long loop to the west with a group of houses on the high bank on the right side. The river begins to widen again and the current slows as the landing at Hinsons Cross Roads nears. Just above the landing is an island. The landing is on the east bank at the end of the island.

Hinsons Cross Roads to Boynton Cutoff Boat Ramp (J–K): 15 miles

DIFFICULTY: Easy
SCENERY: Good
COUNTIES: Holmes, Washington, Walton

ACCESS: From Bonifay, travel south on S.R. 79 to the intersection with S.R. 280. Turn right (west) on S.R. 280 and continue to its junction with S.R. 170. Turn right (west) and continue for less than one mile to the community of Hinsons Cross Roads. Continue west on this road after the pavement ends for two miles to a concrete boat ramp on the river. (See map on page 43.)

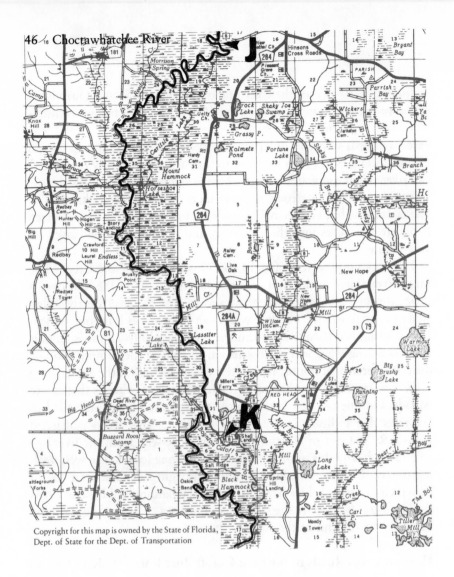

TRIP DESCRIPTION: The river continues to be wide at this point with a good current. The banks continue to be heavily wooded, some four to six feet high. The run from Morrison Spring enters the river from the west about two miles below this put-in. It is one mile up this run to the spring which is a 250-foot pool containing three cavities in the bottom. One of the cavities is said to be 50 feet deep, another is 100 feet deep, and a third is 300 feet deep. All three terminate in a large underground cavern of unknown dimensions. This is a popular spot for swimming and picnicking as well as for diving. There's a concession, pumps for air tanks, and a boat ramp.

A mile below the confluence of the spring run, a large power line crosses the river resulting in a partially cleared high area. There is also a dirt track on the west bank for about a half mile below the power line. This is one of the only high, cleared areas on this section of the river.

Below Morrison Spring, the river makes several large oxbow bends. Sandy Creek enters from the west side midway down one of the straighter sections. This creek is fed from Ponce de Leon Springs some five miles to the north. Just below Sandy Creek, there's a group of large houses on the west bank with no public access.

Less than one-half mile below the houses is a large island. The best run appears to be to the east, but the shortest route is west. Below the island small bayous begin to appear along with an occasional hunting-fishing camp. About three miles below the island, the river takes a sharp turn to the south and begins a long, straight run. These long straights, broken by a few bends, will continue to just above Boynton Cutoff. The frequency of houses increases although they tend to be set well back from the river.

At Boynton Cutoff, the main river goes west, to the right, but is narrower than the cutoff. To follow the cutoff, make a turn east. The water is always very swift in the cutoff. Just around the first bend is an old logging bridge that is usually a catchall for large logs and other debris. This bridge should be approached with caution as the water is swift and it may be difficult to find an opening. Around the next bend on the left is the take-out at a boat ramp on the east side of the river.

TAKE-OUT (K): From Bonifay, travel south on S.R. 79 to the intersection with S.R. 280. Turn right (west) on S.R. 280 and continue to its junction with S.R. 170. Follow S.R. 280/170 to Hinsons Cross Roads. Follow S.R. 284 south from Hinsons Cross Roads for seven miles to the point where S.R. 284 turns due east, but S.R. 284A continues south. Stay on S.R. 284A for just under three miles. Turn right (south) on a graded road and continue to the boat ramp. If you miss this turn, the S.R. 284A will continue for one-half mile to Shell Landing, a boat ramp on Holmes Creek.

When the Boynton Cutoff rejoins the Choctawhatchee River, the river becomes very broad and is frequented by large motorboats. It is seven miles downstream to the bridge at S.R. 20.

Holmes Creek

According to the map, Holmes Creek begins near the Alabama-Florida line, northeast of the town of Bonifay. It is a tiny, unnavigable stream until two miles above Vernon, where the input from Beckton and Cypress Springs increases it into a canoeable waterway. Except in periods of heavy rainfall, Holmes Creek tends to be clear and green. There is a wide variety of trees and the colorful reflections of many different hues of leaves and foliage in the clear water makes this a most photogenic stream.

Beginning and ending in areas of high banks, the middle part of the Holmes Creek trail is through swamps characterized by many sloughs and bayous. Paddling into these by water can also provide an interesting experience. There are also several small springs and creeks that feed Holmes Creek.

Trees along the banks and in the swamps include pine, a variety of oaks, magnolia, cypress, maple, sweet and black gums, and a number of others indigenous to north Florida. Alligators can be observed as well as turtles, raccoons, otters, and skunks. This stream is well known for good fishing in all seasons. The primary fish caught are bream, shellcracker, and crappie.

Holmes Creek has a low gradient and a lazy to almost nonexistent current. There are a few scattered houses on the higher banks, but overall the atmosphere is one of remoteness. It is a very pretty creek, easy to paddle and with good access. It makes an excellent one-day trip and would be pleasant for a leisurely overnight trip if the camper is aware that campsites are somewhat scarce.

Although Holmes Creek flows into the Choctawhatchee River, canoeists usually prefer to take out about three miles above the confluence. It is another six miles to the next access and this section of the Choctawhatchee is popular with large motorboats.

Wayside Park at Vernon, off State Road 79 to Reedy Branch (A–B): 10 miles

DIFFICULTY: Easy
SCENERY: Excellent
COUNTY: Washington

ACCESS: From Vernon travel one-half mile north on S.R. 79, cross the bridge, and turn right at a wayside park on the east side of the road. Access is via a public boat ramp.

TRIP DESCRIPTION: The stream is wide at the access with high banks and some houses for the first few miles. A little over five miles downstream is a boat ramp with a short dock on the east bank. This is the site of Blue Spring. About 60 by 120 feet, and 7 to 10 feet deep, the spring emerges from a limestone cavity near the pool surface at the northeast end. This is a possible site for camping.

Reedy Branch to State Road 284 (Millers Ferry Bridge) (B–C): 8 miles

DIFFICULTY: Easy
SCENERY: Excellent
COUNTY: Washington

ACCESS: From Vernon, travel southwest on S.R. 79 for six miles. Turn right onto a graded road and proceed for just over one mile. A small church will be seen on the right with a dirt road running beside it. Turn right onto this road and continue for less than one mile to Holmes Creek. This access is unimproved and up a 25-foot bluff, but it is not very difficult to put canoes in or out of the creek. It is a possible campsite.

TRIP DESCRIPTION: In this section, the stream continues to alternate between high banks and swampy areas. Reedy Branch flows in from the east just minutes below the put-in and Shaky Joe Branch merges from the west one mile downstream. This section has so many sloughs and backwaters that it is difficult to distinguish between them and in-flowing branches and streams.

Millers Ferry Bridge (State Road 284) to Shell Landing (C–D): 2.5 miles

DIFFICULTY: Easy
SCENERY: Good
COUNTY: Washington

ACCESS: From Vernon, travel southwest on S.R. 79 seven miles to the intersection with S.R. 284. Turn right (west) on 284 and continue just

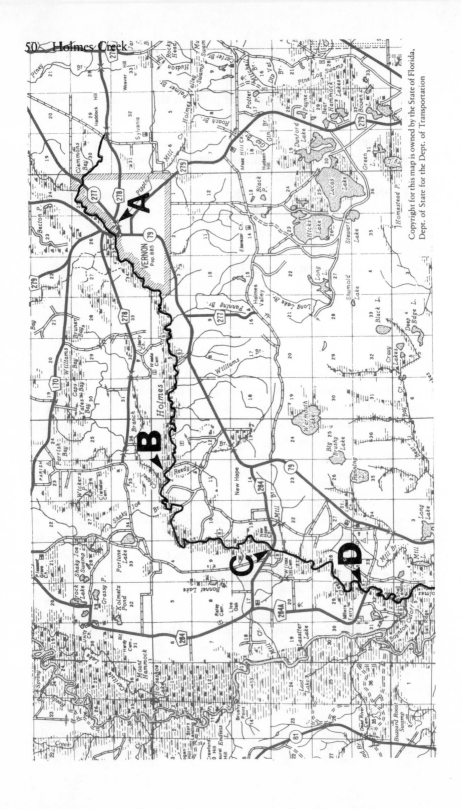

over two miles to the bridge across Holmes Creek. A privately owned ramp is located about fifty yards west of the bridge.

TRIP DESCRIPTION: This section is similar to, but less swampy than, those described earlier. At the take-out, Holmes Creek is less than a mile upstream from the Boynton Cutoff section of the Choctawhatchee River and two miles from the confluence of the two waterways.

TAKE-OUT (D): From Vernon, travel southwest on S.R. 79 seven miles to the junction of S.R. 284. Turn right (west) and continue for less than four miles to the junction with S.R. 284A. Turn left (south) on S.R. 284A and continue for three miles to Shell Landing, a boat ramp on Holmes Creek.

Econfina Creek

Many canoeists consider Econfina Creek to be the most beautiful and challenging stream in Florida; undoubtedly, it is one of the most unique and unpredictable. The upper section of the creek drains 1,240 square miles of sandy, porous soil through a steep, narrow ravine with a gradient of more than five feet per mile. The unusual composition of the soils in this area has permitted this creek to cut deep canyons some fifteen feet high that result in exciting chutes of rapidly cascading water. It is the only stream in Florida that is recommended for *experienced canoeists only*.

On the lower section, Econfina Creek is fed by a number of outstanding springs. The Gainer Springs group consists of three major springs that constitute one of Florida's twenty-seven first magnitude springs. In addition, there is a bevy of other minor springs along the banks. Blue Springs, Williford Springs, Walsingham Spring, and Pitt Springs are among those that have been named. Spectacular Emerald Springs discharges from a 25-foot-tall limestone bank and is part of an area that is being acquired for use as a state park. This section of the creek is an easy run and is frequented by tubers in the summertime.

The very high banks on Econfina Creek may be yellow sand bluffs up to 50 feet tall, or beautiful limestone walls, dripping with ferns. Many plants native to the Appalachian Mountains are seen along the banks. Dogwood, redbud, masses of mountain laurel, and several varieties of wild azalea make it a garden in the spring. Oak-leaf hydrangea grows in the crevices of the limestone walls and spills white flowers down the banks throughout the summer months.

Trees commonly seen include beech, cedar, sweet gum, holly, magnolia, red maple, cypress, and Carolina silver bell as well as various types of pine and oak. Glimpses of wildlife are hard to catch because of the high banks, but deer, raccoon, otter, bobcat, fox, and beaver are indigenous to the area.

Because it is generally very shallow in the upper section, the canoeist can expect a number of pull-overs. Stobs, logs, and rock ledges are to be avoided and sharp bends to be maneuvered. At high water, the combination of these obstructions with very fast current can be extremely hazardous. The drainage-ditch nature of this creek makes it prone to flash flooding and it is absolutely essential to stay off the stream at high water or if thunderstorms are predicted.

Access to Econfina Creek is limited and the surrounding area is undeveloped. This provides a pleasant wilderness experience, but also makes rescue lengthy and difficult.

There are water gauges at Scotts Bridge and Walsingham Bridge. At one time there was a metal plate on Scotts Bridge to assist in interpreting the gauge reading. It has been removed, but the plate read:

1–2 ft.	(low water) 50 logjams—15 hrs. paddling time.
2–4 ft.	(normal) 24 logjams—12 hrs. paddling time.
4–9 ft.	(high water) Very fast water, 12 logjams and 11 hrs. paddling time. Experienced canoeist only.
9 ft. or more.	(flood stage) Stay off the river.

Even though it is only 22 miles, paddling the run on Econfina Creek in one day is not recommended. It is possible to make a comfortable one-day trip by taking out at Walsingham Bridge. The road to the bridge is frequently in extremely poor condition however, and it is best not to plan to use it without scouting in advance.

The high banks and lack of sandbars make choosing a campsite a challenge on Econfina. There are a number of excellent spots high off the river in the beech woods. Beech trees have widespread branches that discourage ground cover. As a result, nice clearings, perfect for campsites, can often be found under them. Firewood is also plentiful in the area.

Econfina is a Muskogean Indian word that is said to mean *natural bridge*. Evidently there was such a bridge on this creek near the site where S.R. 20 now crosses the stream. No evidence of it remains. There is another stream of the same name, but pronounced differently, about one hundred miles east, between St. Marks and Perry. This Econfina Creek rhymes with "shiner." Econfina River in Taylor County rhymes with "beaner."

Scotts Bridge to Walsingham Bridge (A–B): 10 miles

DIFFICULTY: Strenuous
SCENERY: Superb
COUNTIES: Bay, Washington

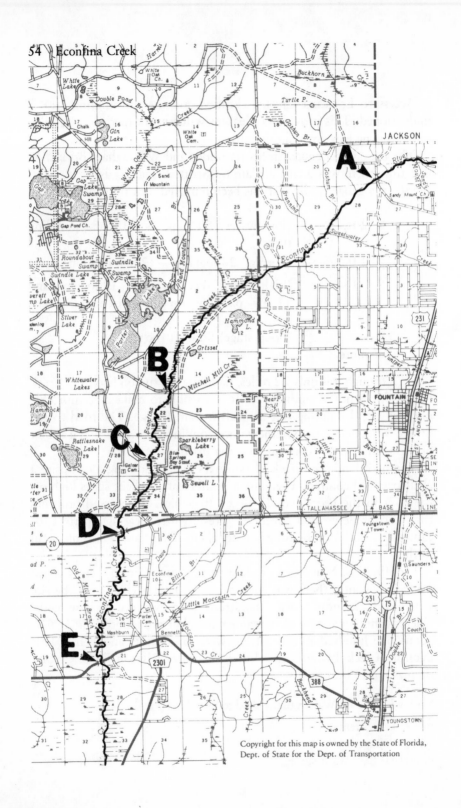

ACCESS: From Fountain, travel U.S. 231 north for 4 miles to the junction of U.S. 231 and S.R. 167. Continue less than one-half mile to a wide, graded road that turns left—Scott road. Turn left (west) on Scott road follow it a little over two miles to the wooden bridge. Put in on the north side of the road on either side of the bridge.

TRIP DESCRIPTION: The river, 15 to 20 feet wide, is generally shallow and swift at this point. Some small sandbars are on the first few bends and usually a pull-over is around the second bend.

Very soon, the stream begins to twist and turn with drops over submerged tree trunks and rocky ledges. The banks are from four to six feet high, canopied with trees, and in some places the stream is hardly wider than the canoe. For the next four miles, the creek has intermittent high-walled flumes interspersed with very short stretches of flatter, shallower water. Trees that have fallen across the creek can be very hazardous in the narrow, swift chutes.

About four miles above Walsingham Bridge, the banks begin to drop somewhat and the stream becomes wider and shallower. This results in a great many obstructions in the water, such as fallen trees, and large limbs, many of which must be pulled over; this is especially true in low water.

A high sandbank on the east side of the river marks the beginning of some strenuous canoeing. A primitive road leads to the sandbank and some canoeists, equipped with an off-road vehicle and a winch, take out here. At low water, the next two miles will have numerous pull-overs.

The remainder of the trip to Walsingham Bridge is spaced with some shallow spots and some sections where the water is three to four feet deep. The run from an unnamed spring flows into the creek from the east bank.

Walsingham Bridge to Blue Springs (B–C): 3 miles

DIFFICULTY: Moderate
SCENERY: Good
COUNTY: Washington

ACCESS: From Fountain, travel north on U.S. 231 for 2 miles to a graded road on the left. Turn left on Owenwood road travel two and one-half miles to Deep Springs road. Turn left and go one-half mile to the first road on the right, Brown road. Turn right and continue until you reach Walsingham Bridge. After the first two miles this road becomes little more than a dirt track, and is five miles of deep sand through remote woods.

TRIP DESCRIPTION: From Walsingham Bridge to Blue Springs is a less interesting section of Econfina Creek. There is a small spring, Walsingham Spring, on the west bank about a quarter mile below the bridge and another spring that boils up in the river another half mile down. Mitchell Mill Creek flows in from the east bank just below the bridge.

The stream is wider, the banks lower, and there are several pull-overs at normal-water level. A few houses appear on the east bank one mile above Blue Springs, a recreation area.

Blue Springs is not visible from the river and is reached by paddling up the spring run, or by beaching at the point where the run flows into the river. Coming downstream, watch for a cleared area that may still have rustic benches and evidence of picnics. The run enters on the east bank among some juniper stumps in the river. It may be necessary to lift your canoe over the remains of a crude dam. Paddle upstream 150 yards and another spring run will enter from the left. Again you may have to lift over a beaver dam. There are two caves in the Blue Springs pool. The water is a clear, powder blue. This property, formerly used as a Boy Scout Camp, is owned by a large paper company. Blue Springs has been recently closed (1984) to vehicle traffic, but it is still possible to take out here by carrying canoes and gear some 100 yards to a nearby road. This access may be completely closed in the future.

Blue Springs to State Road 20 (C–D): 3 miles

DIFFICULTY: Moderate
SCENERY: Excellent
COUNTIES: Washington, Bay

ACCESS: From Fountain travel south on U.S. 231 for 2 miles to the intersection with S.R. 20. Turn right (west) and travel to where Blue Springs road, a graded road with a sign, turns north. Follow that road to the entrance to Blue Springs. It is no longer possible to drive directly to the access point. Canoeists have been permitted to continue to take out here by carrying their canoes some 100 yards to a nearby road. Check to see if this is permitted before using this access.

TRIP DESCRIPTION: This section of the river is similar to Section B–C, but it becomes swampier. Several springs, including Williford, Pitt, and a number of unnamed springs, enter from the west bank. Spring runs are easily determined by the clear blue or green water that flows into the creek. The property around these springs may be fenced and guarded. On warm weekends, you may be approached by a guard if you paddle up the runs. Remain in your canoes, be pleasant, and leave promptly if you should be asked to do so.

State Road 20 to State Road 388 (Bennett Bridge) (D–E): 6 miles

DIFFICULTY: Easy
SCENERY: Excellent
COUNTY: Bay

ACCESS: From Fountain travel south on U.S. 231 for 2 miles to the intersection with S.R. 20. Turn right (west) on S.R. 20 and travel 7 miles to the bridge across S.R. 20. Access is on the northeast side.

TRIP DESCRIPTION: At this point Econfina Creek becomes accessible to small motorboats and is heavily populated by persons in inner tubes; thus it loses some of its wilderness flavor. It is a worthwhile trip, however, if only to see the springs and the intermittent low swamplands and high limestone banks.

The Gainer Springs begin within one mile of S.R. 20 and are located on both banks. Emerald Springs, the most spectacular of this group is on the west bank and discharge from under a 25 foot limestone bank. Directly across the creek, a spring run from the east bank leads to a number of springs also. Watch the coloration of the water for evidence of a spring or spring run. These springs are on private property and may be guarded. Again, stay in your canoe and leave promptly and pleasantly if asked to do so.

The section of Econfina Creek below the Bennett bridge is accessible to large motorboats and is also a route for boat traffic to Deer Point Lake. It is not usually of interest to canoeists.

TAKE-OUT (E): From Fountain travel 7 miles south to the intersection of U.S. 231 and S.R. 20. Travel west on S.R. 20 for just over six miles to a graded road that turns left (south). Turn left, and continue on this road for three miles until it joins S.R. 388. At S.R. 388, turn right and continue for one and one-half miles to Econfina Creek. Cross the creek;

the access is a quarter of a mile west of the bridge off a graded road that leads back to the stream. There is an undeveloped camping area at this access that is heavily used in warm weather. From the town of Youngstown, travel west on S.R. 388 for 10 miles to Econfina Creek. Cross the creek; the access is a quarter of a mile west of the bridge off a graded road that leads back to the stream.

Chipola River

The Chipola River rises in southeast Alabama and flows southward 80 miles to the Apalachicola River. In between, it goes underground, flows through a state park, and becomes part of Dead Lake. Over 50 miles of it is a canoe trail that varies from sections of swift, tree-lined, limestone creek to a broad, slow-moving stream with occasional bluffs, cliffs, and caves. It also offers options of a hazardous log canal, a rapid, and many springs and tributaries to explore.

The Chipola becomes navigable just above the S.R. 162 bridge in northern Jackson County with the confluence of Cowarts Creek, Marshall Creek, and Hays Spring Run. It picks up momentum with the addition of several small streams as well as Waddells Mill Creek and goes underground at Florida Caverns State Park. A logging canal can carry the adventurous one-half mile over the natural bridge to the river rise.

Although the Chipola has an aura of remoteness, it runs through heavily populated agricultural areas and except in the extreme lower section, the river is never far from fields, farms, and paved roads. The river usually varies from a smokey green to a clear emerald green depending on rainfall, runoff, and siltation. In periods of heavy rainfall it will be a muddy yellow or tan due to runoff from the red clay topsoil of the surrounding agricultural lands.

Since the terrain on the Chipola varies from high bluffs and sandy hills to lowland swamps, there is a wide variety of trees and vegetation. Almost every kind of tree indigenous to north Florida can be seen. Flowering plants include wild azalea, honeysuckle, daisies of various hues, and the spectacular cardinal flower. Alligators and turtles are the most commonly seen animals but deer, raccoons, opossums, and turkeys can also be found.

The Chipola is noted for good fishing with catfish, bream, bass, and even mullet being caught. The bird life is extremely abundant and the lower section of the river is especially suited to birdwatching.

Because the Chipola does not have sandbars and the lower banks tend to be swampy, good campsites are not plentiful. Much of it is private property as well. Watch for areas that have obviously been used as hunting or fishing camps and that do not have no trespassing signs. Property belonging to the paper companies may also be used for camp-

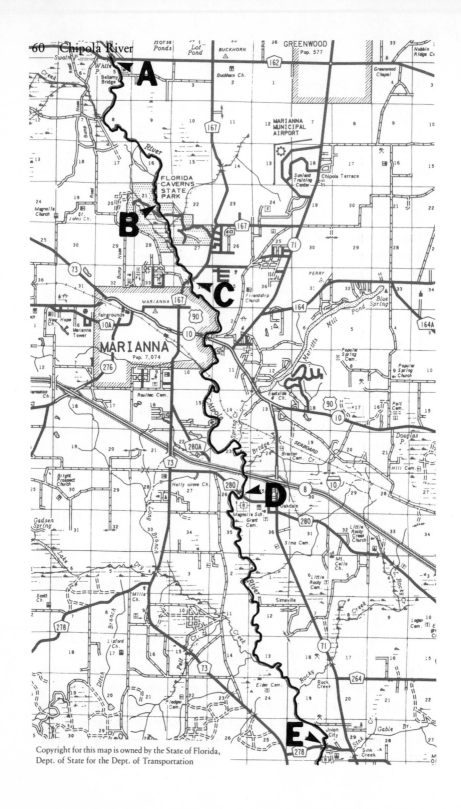

ing, but be careful with campfires and litter to insure that this generous policy stays in effect.

The Chipola is especially suited for canoe trips of several days duration, but access points are also located at convenient intervals for day trips.

State Road 162 to Florida Caverns State Park (A–B): 5 miles

DIFFICULTY: Moderate
SCENERY: Excellent
COUNTY: Jackson

ACCESS: From the town of Greenwood, travel west on S.R. 162 until the bridge over the Chipola River is reached. The put-in is on the southwest side of the bridge.

TRIP DESCRIPTION: This section of the river tends to be tan and shallow at normal-water levels. The banks are low and swampy for the first mile. The remains of Bellamy Bridge cross the river about one-half mile below the put-in. This is a historic road and the site of the bridge is a short distance west of the location of the Bellamy Plantation, a pre-Civil War farm with a colorful history.

The run from Waddells Mill Creek enters the Chipola about one and one-half miles from S.R. 162. This millpond is formed from Rockarch Spring, a second magnitude spring, and is a site that was frequented by the Chatot Indians. It is listed in the National Register of Historic Places. Baker Creek, a tributary of Waddells Mill Creek is also spring fed by Daniel, Tanner, Webbville, and several unnamed springs.

After the confluence of Waddells Mill Creek, the Chipola widens considerably and is similar to a narrow lake for about one-half mile. It narrows again and continues through a low, swampy area with numerous bends. The low banks in this area permit the canoeist to paddle along at eye level with the surrounding swamps and forests.

One mile above Florida Caverns State Park, Bosel Spring run enters the river from the east bank. The main spring is about two-tenths of a mile up the run and is a 50-foot pool with three narrow vents about 25 feet deep. The water is a clear blue, offset by bright green water weeds. There are three other spring pools in the Bosel group, all separated by natural bridges.

A boat ramp is located at the state park where the river goes underground. For the adventurous, there is an old canal dug for the purposes of floating logs down the river to river rise, where the river seeps back up from underground. It is one-half mile long, extremely narrow, and frequently choked with trees, logs, and the remains of old boats. At high water it is dangerously fast and technical, at low water there are many pull-overs.

Most canoeists choose to take out at the boat ramp at the state park and resume their trip at S.R. 167.

When using the state park for launching, don't forget that the gates are closed at sundown, a variable time, according to the season of the year. Be sure and check with the ranger to find out what time the gates will be locked.

State Road 167 to State Road 280A (Magnolia Bridge) (C–D): 10 miles

DIFFICULTY: Moderate
SCENERY: Excellent
COUNTY: Jackson

ACCESS: From the town of Marianna, travel north on S.R. 167 to the bridge across the Chipola River. Access is on the southwest side at a public boat ramp.

TRIP DESCRIPTION: For those who do not choose to run the log canal through the state park, it is a two-mile paddle upstream to the river rise. This is not a dramatic sight, however, as the river seems to seep back through the woods rather than rising in any one clearly defined spot. The run from Blue Hole Spring also flows into the river in this section, but having traversed almost two miles of swamp, it has lost its clarity and is not easily identified.

Going downriver from S.R. 167, the banks continue to be low and swampy with some limestone in evidence. Less than a half mile below the S.R. 167 put-in, the run from Sand Bag Springs enters from the west bank. It is 50 yards up the run to the spring which is located on private property, and is usually indistinguishable from the river.

The Chipola flows under U.S. 90 two miles down from S.R. 167 but there is not a good access to the river at that point. This section of the stream tends to be littered due to the proximity of the town of Marianna and heavy usage.

Just at the edge of the city limits of Marianna and about one mile below U.S. 90, the Louisville and Nashville Railroad tracks cross the Chipola. The west bank is very high at this point with a grotto carved out of the limestone that is partially the result of a natural cave and partially man-made by limestone having been removed for building purposes. A pretty little pool at the bottom of this bluff appears to be a miniature quarry as well as a spring.

The limestone wall continues along the west bank of the river for another one-half mile to the opening of a large cavern known locally as Alamo Cave. At low water, one can walk into the cave, which is said to penetrate deeply into the hillside. Shortly below the cave, a spring run enters from the east bank. Seventy-five yards up the run is a small, deep pool created by Dykes Spring; a couple of well-used campsites are at this spot.

Approximately six miles down, a major tributary of the Chipola, Spring Creek, enters from the east. Spring Creek is the run from Merritts Mill Pond which is fed by one first magnitude and several second magnitude springs.

The head spring for Merritts Mill Pond is Blue Spring. One of Florida's largest and more popular springs, the area is underlain by caves and tunnels hundreds of feet long with depths approaching 300 feet. There is a second spring 300 feet downstream and another 1,000 feet to the south. Numerous other springs are said to flow into the four mile long lake that ends at a dam at U.S. 90. Spring Creek begins just below the dam and flows about two miles to the Chipola River. This is an alternative put-in for a Chipola River trip and well worth seeing. Due to the shallow water and swift current, it is difficult to paddle upstream from the Chipola into Spring Creek for any distance.

At low water, there will be several rocky shoals in the one mile from the mouth of Spring Creek to Interstate 10. The take-out at S.R. 280A is less than a mile downstream from the interstate on the southwest side of the bridge.

State Road 280A to State Road 278 (D–E): 10 miles

DIFFICULTY: Easy
SCENERY: Good
COUNTY: Jackson

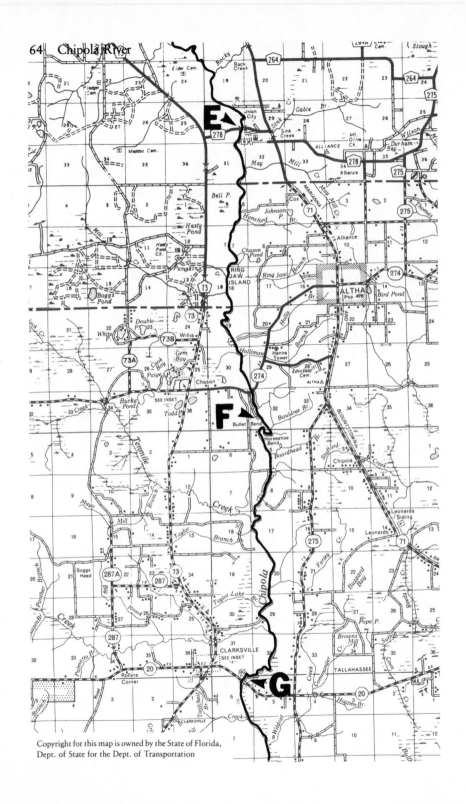

Copyright for this map is owned by the State of Florida,
Dept. of State for the Dept. of Transportation

ACCESS: From Mariana travel south on S.R. 71 to the intersection with Interstate 10. Continue for less than one-half mile to the first paved road turning right, S.R. 280A. Turn right and continue for one mile to the river. Access is on the southwest side of the bridge.

TRIP DESCRIPTION: This is a pleasant trip with steep, sloping banks and a number of small, rocky shoals. The river splits to run around several small islands with good runs on both sides. The current tends to be moderate to slow most of the way, but picks up on the shoals.

Dry Creek enters the Chipola about seven miles from this access. This very long creek flows into the river from ten miles to the west and is fed by a number of smaller creeks as well as by Spring Lake. This lake is fed by at least four springs including Springboard, Mill Pond, Double, and Gadsen. Dry Creek is reported to be canoeable in wet weather. There are perhaps a dozen houses on this section but they are scattered in such a manner as not to intrude on the feeling of remoteness.

State Road 278 to State Road 274 (E–F): 8 miles

DIFFICULTY: Easy
SCENERY: Good
COUNTIES: Jackson, Calhoun

ACCESS: From Marianna travel south on S.R. 71 for six miles past the interstate to the junction of S.R. 278. Turn right (west) on S.R. 278 and travel one-half mile to the river.

TRIP DESCRIPTION: This eight-mile section is similar to those described earlier. Sink Creek enters from the east just minutes below the put-in and Ring Jaw Island and shoals are four miles downstream. The soft limestone bottom that is evident on most of the Chipola is especially obvious on this section.

Sizable cracks in the riverbed can be seen when the water is clear and a number of oddly shaped rocks, such as Table Rock, attest to the power of the water on the soft strata.

State Road 274 to State Road 20 (F–G): 10 miles

DIFFICULTY: Easy
SCENERY: Good
COUNTY: Calhoun

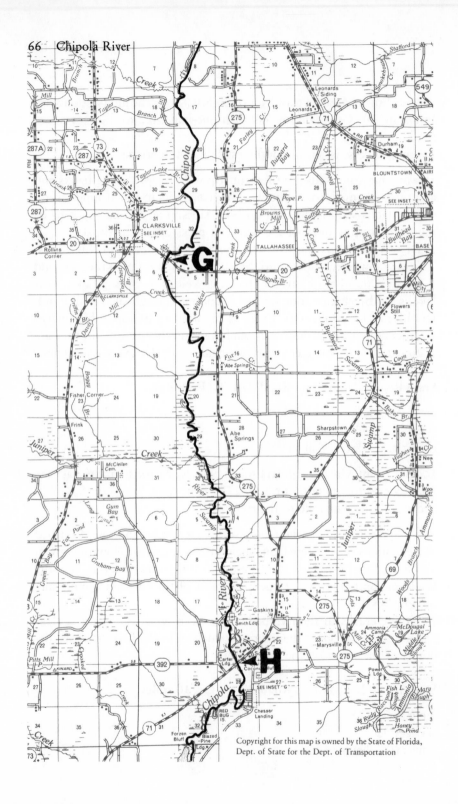

Copyright for this map is owned by the State of Florida, Dept. of State for the Dept. of Transportation

ACCESS: From Mariana travel south of S.R. 71 for 11 miles past the interstate to the junction of S.R. 274. Turn right (west) and continue for four miles to the bridge. The access is off a dirt road that runs beside the river on the west bank.

TRIP DESCRIPTION: This is one of the most popular runs on the Chipola due to the presence of Look and Tremble Rapid, a limestone shoal that crosses the river just below the S.R. 274 bridge. The dirt road beside the river provides easy access to the rapid which is a popular picnic spot as well as providing sport for tubers and swimmers.

At normal-water levels, the rapid has a small standing wave at the bottom and a minor hydraulic. It should be run on the east bank, or in high water through the middle.

For the first five miles below the rapid, the banks tend to be vertical limestone six to eight feet high. Tenmile Creek flows in from the west through high limestone walls and is canoeable in wet weather.

About halfway down this section, the banks become lower and more gentle with only a few high bluffs. Fourmile Creek enters from the west. The current is usually helpful on this section but slows as the river becomes deeper and broader shortly above S.R. 20. There are a number of houses visible from the river and several boat landings and other access points. It is an easy and pleasant float trip with the rapids to lend interest. Campsites are limited due to the high banks and presence of houses and private landowners.

State Road 20 to State Road 71 (G–H): 13 miles

DIFFICULTY: Easy
SCENERY: Excellent
COUNTY: Calhoun

ACCESS: From Blountstown, travel west for six miles on S.R. 20 to the bridge across the Chipola River. Access is at a paved boat ramp and wayside park on the northwest bank.

TRIP DESCRIPTION: The character of the Chipola undergoes a radical change in this section as it leaves the high lands and descends into the swamps. For several miles below S.R. 20, the high banks and limestone bottom continue, but after the advent of Fox Creek from the east, the banks begin to lower and the nature of the vegetation begins to change. Patches of saw grass and lily pads appear and the less is seen of oaks and pines and more of tupelo and cypress with some sycamore and cedar.

Juniper Creek, a sometimes canoeable stream, enters from the west five miles down and beyond that point the river becomes even swampier. Sloughs and bayous become more numerous and the current is slower. About three miles above S.R. 71, the river splits and flows into a thick swamp called Ward Lake. Following the current will eventually lead directly to the bridge. Don't wander too far into the swamp unless it is early in the day and you have a compass.

Wildlife is abundant on this section and includes alligators, otters, turtles, water birds, and ducks in season. Fishing is said to be excellent and catches include bass, bream, catfish, and trout. Deer, raccoons, opossums, and other animals indigenous to this area are common in the woods. Camping would be possible in the first two miles, but campsites are scarce after that.

TAKE-OUT (H): From Blountstown, travel south on S.R. 71 for 16 miles to the bridge across the Chipola River.

The Chipola River continues through a swampy area for several miles until it runs into Dead Lake. After traversing the lake for seven or eight miles, it regroups and flows south through a very large swamp for another ten miles until it flows into the Apalachicola River. It is considered unwise to travel the Dead Lake or the lower section of the river without a guide. Due to the distance, lack of access, and lack of campsites, it also is not appropriate for most canoeists.

Rivers of the Central Panhandle

Wacissa River

Photograph by Slim Ray

Streams in the Apalachicola National Forest

The Apalachicola National Forest covers 59,000 acres of the Gulf Coastal Lowlands west of Tallahassee to Bristol, and expands southward to within a few miles of the coast. It abounds in lakes, rivers and streams appropriate for canoeing as well as sinkholes, wilderness and scenic areas, and archeological sites. It provides habitat for six rare or endangered species, including the Southern bald eagle, the red-cockaded woodpecker, the sandhill crane, the osprey, the Florida panther, and the alligator.

Forest roads are graded sand or clay and except for some major thoroughfares, tend to be poorly maintained and remote. As a result, some of the most interesting places in the forest are difficult to reach. Rivers, creeks, swamps, and bogs also limit accessability sometimes necessitating long shuttles on doubtful roads. The lower sections of the Ochlockonee River are in the forest and the Sopchoppy River, New River, and Lost Creek are almost completely within its boundaries, as are Fisher Creek, and Bradford Brook. Telogia Creek, which flows southward into the Ochlockonee through a narrow corridor of land surrounded by, but not a part of, the national forest will be mentioned in this section.

Because of their inaccessibility to the general population and/or extreme dependency on perfect water conditions for enjoyable canoeing, most of the national forest streams will not be discussed in detail. Brief information will be given on Fisher Creek, Bradford Brook, New River, and Telogia Creek. The Sopchoppy River and Lost Creek will be discussed in more detail, and the Ochlockonee River, which is only incidentally in the forest, will be treated in a separate section.

Sopchoppy River

The Sopchoppy River drains from a large swamp south of Lake Talquin and flows for 50 miles to its confluence with the Ochlockonee at Ochlockonee Bay. Lying almost completely within the boundaries of the Apalachicola National Forest, it is an unusually remote and clean river. Sopchoppy is a Creek Indian word said to mean *long twisted stream*, an apt description of this beautiful waterway. In addi-

71

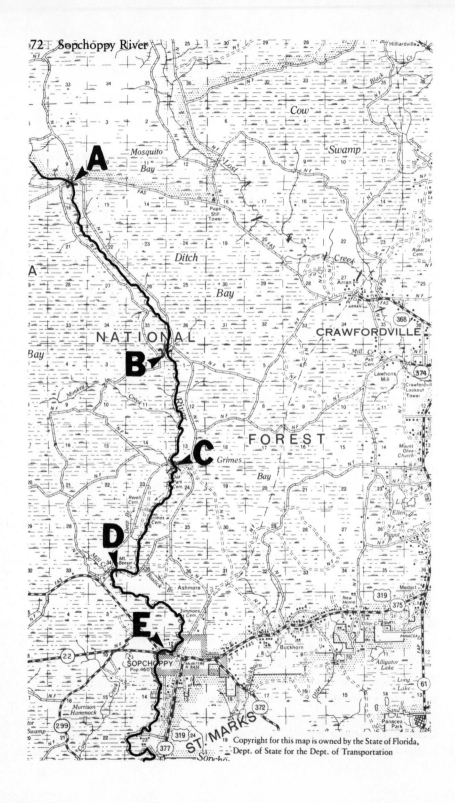

Copyright for this map is owned by the State of Florida,
Dept. of State for the Dept. of Transportation

tion to its many twists and turns, the Sopchoppy is noted for extensive and very unique cypress formations, high limestone banks, and an overall fast current.

Highly dependent on local rainfall for its flow, the Sopchoppy can be either low stretches connecting deeper pools during dry periods or a rushing ten-foot channel after heavy rains. In either event, the sharp bends and presence of cypress knees in the water can present a challenge to the canoeist.

The riverbed is primarily sand with some rock crevices; the water is a clear, but highly colored, tannic red. The high banks are occasionally broken by white sandbars suitable for picnicking or camping.

Of special interest on the Sopchoppy is the Bradwell Bay. A virtually undisturbed scenic area, it escaped the lumbering craze of a half-century ago and harbors a number of award-winning trees. There are also 17 archeologically valuable sites along the river that are said to be the only models of aboriginal usages of the flatwoods in northwest Florida. A number of endangered species including the Florida panther, the red-cockaded woodpecker, and the Southern bald eagle make their homes in the area. The black bear, a Florida-designated threatened species, is also a native of these forests.

Vegetation is dense along the banks and includes loblolly pine forests, pine-palmetto flatwoods, cypress, titi, and other trees indigenous to the area. The steep limestone banks are covered with mosses and ferns and in the spring wild azaleas provide a canopy of pink bloom.

Forest Road 13 to Forest Road 129 (A–B): 10 miles

DIFFICULTY: Moderate to Strenuous
SCENERY: Excellent
COUNTY: Wakulla

ACCESS: From the town of Crawfordville, travel west on S.R. 368. Continue until the pavement ends and then continue on the graded road for about seven more miles to the bridge across the Sopchoppy River.

TRIP DESCRIPTION: This section of the river begins at the most southern edge of the Grand Bay swamp whose runoff forms the river. It is said to be possible to canoe one bridge farther, but high water and a lot of bushwhacking is required. The river is clearly defined at the F.R. 13 bridge, but fingers off into a swampy area for about one-half mile downstream. Despite the swampy terrain, the current is easily detectable and will lead to a well-defined channel with banks from one to three feet high.

Very sharp twists and turns in a narrow streambed characterize this part of the river. Cypress knees and the remains of downed trees and stumps contribute to the obstructions that must be avoided. The constant curves and swift water leave little opportunity to scout as immediate decisions are required in maneuvering. This section of the river should only be run at high water. The gauge at the Mt. Beeser bridge should read at least ten feet.

Forest Rd. 129 to Forest Rd. 346 (Oak Park Bridge) (B–C): 5 miles

DIFFICULTY: Moderate
SCENERY: Excellent
COUNTY: Wakulla

ACCESS: From the town of Crawfordville, travel west on S.R. 368 for about three miles. F.R. 365 will intersect from an angle on the left. Turn left, and continue for another three miles. F.R. 348 will intersect from the right. Turn right and travel two and one-half miles to the intersection of F.R. 329 on the left. Turn left and the bridge will be in sight.

TRIP DESCRIPTION: A very popular section of river for canoeing, the Middle Sopchoppy is noted for the wide diversity of beautiful and unique cypress formations. In addition to a multitude of knees of all sizes and shapes, there are long, flowing banks of cypress wood, connecting groups of knees that resemble entwined serpents, monsters, gargoyles, or whatever the active imagination can envision.

The sharp bends in the river are frequently obstructed by masses of cypress knees resulting in small rapids and falls that require fast maneuvering. There are several small sandbars in this section that are pleasant for lunching, camping, or sunbathing.

Forest Road 346 (Oak Park bridge) to Forest Road 365 (Mt. Beeser bridge) (C–D): 5 miles

DIFFICULTY: Moderate
SCENERY: Good
COUNTY: Wakulla

ACCESS: From the town of Sopchoppy, travel northwest on S.R. 375 for about two miles. Turn right on F.R. 346 and continue for less than a mile, turn right and cross the Mt. Beeser bridge. Continue to the dead end, turn left on F.R. 348B and travel north for about four miles to the intersection with F.R. 346. Turn left and proceed to the Oak Park bridge.

When coming down Section B–C, from the bridge on F.R. 129, retrace to the point where 348B branches to the right. Turn right and continue to the point where F.R. 346 intersects to the right. Turn right and continue to the Oak Park bridge.

TRIP DESCRIPTION: From just above the Oak Park bridge, the river has begun to widen and the curves have become more gentle. High, limestone banks begin to be evident and there are several small islands that narrow the channels of the river. The vertical banks act as a watershed and in warm weather produce a cooling effect. In the winter they may be dripping with icicles. The river is deeper and easier to negotiate in this section but still requires some skill.

Just before the Mt. Beeser bridge, the river leaves the national forest and houses and other forms of encroachment appear. Small motorboats may also be seen near the end of this section.

Mt. Beeser Bridge to State Route 375 (D–E): 5 miles

DIFFICULTY: Easy
SCENERY: Good
COUNTY: Wakulla

ACCESS: From the town of Sopchoppy travel northwest on S.R. 375 for about two miles. Turn right on F.R. 346 for less than a mile and turn right. The Mt. Beeser bridge is within sight.

TRIP DESCRIPTION: The Sopchoppy River becomes deeper, slower, and increasingly populated beyond this point. It moves from the swamps and upland hardwoods, to a more marshy, coastal appearance.

It is possible to continue to paddle on the Sopchoppy to U.S. 319 (about four miles), to the city park at Sopchoppy, and even to its confluence with the Ocholockonee. It becomes increasingly broad and tidal, however, and is heavily used by motorboats.

TAKE-OUT (E): From the town of Sopchoppy, travel west on S.R. 375 to the bridge across the Sopchoppy River. Access is on the northeast side of the bridge.

Lost Creek

Located entirely within the Apalachicola National Forest, Lost Creek is very similar in terrain and geography to the upper section of the Sopchoppy River which it parallels. It drains some ten miles through Cow Swamp and Mosquito Bay, and disappears into a sink, less than a mile below S.R. 368. It is smaller and more winding than the Sopchoppy. There is little development on Lost Creek and it is a fine example of upland pine woods with a border of cypress and wetlands trees. This waterway is highly dependent on local rainfall.

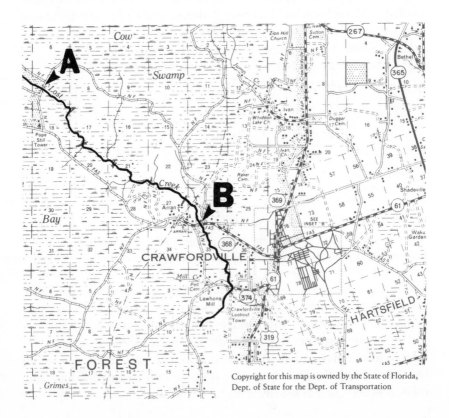

Copyright for this map is owned by the State of Florida, Dept. of State for the Dept. of Transportation

Forest Road 360 to State Road 368 (A–B): 10 miles

DIFFICULTY: Moderate to Strenuous
SCENERY: Excellent
COUNTY: Wakulla

ACCESS: From the town of Crawfordville, travel west on S.R. 368; continue past the end of the pavement to the graded road (now F.R. 13). Shortly beyond the end of the pavement, F.R. 350 angles off to the right. Follow F.R. 350 to the first concrete bridge.

TRIP DESCRIPTION: Lost Creek begins in a swampy area, but by following the current, a clearly defined riverbed will be reached. This is a narrow, twisting stream with many underwater obstructions such as cypress knees and submerged logs and stumps. Good maneuvering skills will be needed. This is a fine example of wilderness paddling. This stream should only be run during times of local high rainfall.

TAKE-OUT (B): From Crawfordville, travel west on S.R. 368 for about two miles to the bridge across Lost Creek. Access is on the southwest side of the bridge.

Other Streams in the Apalachicola National Forest

There are a number of waterways in and close to the national forest that are of interest to canoeists. Unfortunately, some have very long and difficult shuttles, some have many obstacles and possible portages, and some are only navigable for short periods of time under very special weather and water conditions. A brief description of these streams follows, but the canoeist determined to paddle them would be well advised to seek up-to-the-minute information from a local person who is familiar with them.

Telogia Creek, not actually in the national forest, winds south from S.R. 20 in Liberty County to the Ochlockonee River through a corridor of privately owned land bordered to the east and west by the forest. It runs through an extremely remote swampy area and has little high ground and almost no access. While its remoteness makes it abound in wildlife and beautiful and rare vegetation, it is a very difficult and hazardous canoeing experience.

Fisher Creek, only ten miles southwest of Tallahassee in Leon County, drains a series of small lakes on the extreme western edge of the Grand Bay swamp. It is a small, narrow, tightly winding creek that drops off a karst and disappears into a sinkhole. Only five miles long, it has a steep gradient, resulting in very technical canoeing. It is run by the adventurous at very high-water levels.

The New River, of great interest to naturalists, is a worthwhile canoe trip for those experienced in wilderness paddling, who have stamina, and a flexible outlook. It is the last remnant of the famed Tates Hell Swamp in Franklin County and is especially noted for the age and vigor of its tree cover. The Atlantic white cedar, which does not occur east of the New River is abundant in the area and many appear to be virgin stands. The rare white cedar, regrowth of cypress, and an abundance of American holly contribute to the beautiful forestation.

The New River is a small river that flows through bald cypress stands and large titi swamps. It flows from the Brushy Islands area, just south of Telogia Creek, to the Gulf of Mexico at Carrabelle but is frequently lost in swamp. Canoe trips on this river usually originate at Owens Bridge and terminate at Gully Branch. Access to these points is difficult and dependent on good weather conditions. Unfortunately good conditions for paddling the New River require an abundance of rainfall which in turn tends to wash out the roads.

Bradford Brook, on the outskirts of Tallahassee in Leon County, is a chain of cypress-ringed lakes that interconnect. The almost total lack of current makes this a pleasant canoeing experience for beginners and one can paddle in either direction. Under very dry conditions, travel between lakes is difficult.

The Ochlockonee River Basin

One of north Florida's longest rivers, the Ochlockonee begins in Worth County, Georgia, and flows for nearly 150 miles to the Gulf of Mexico near Panacea, Florida. In Georgia, its major tributaries are the West Fork of the Ochlockonee and Barnetts Creek. In Florida it is fed by Telogia Creek and the Little River, but throughout its length it is also the recipient of runoff from hundreds of tiny creeks, streams, and rivulets.

Above Georgia S.R. 93 the stream is narrow and obstructed by deadfalls and willow trees. Below the Ochlockonee River State Park it is as wide as a bay—windy, tidal, and popular with motorboats. For canoeing purposes, the sections from Georgia S.R. 93 to the state park, a distance of 100 miles, are preferred. The upper portion of the river is criss-crossed with access roads—two, four, and ten miles apart.

Below U.S. 90 in Florida, the river flows for nineteen miles through the man-made Lake Talquin. The lake is seldom more than two miles wide, but has many islands, hammocks, and finger lakes that can obscure the canoe trail. Like most lakes, it can be windy with high waves, and is frequented by motorboats. There is also a dam just above S.R. 20 that must be portaged. Most canoeists paddle the Ochlockonee either above or below the lake.

Once it flows out of Lake Talquin, the distances between accesses lengthen. The river flows through the Apalachicola National Forest for over 50 miles with only one bridge and a very limited number of boat landings.

Since the Ochlockonee is prone to extensive flooding, there are few houses or other encroachments along the banks.

Vegetation on the Ochlockonee is characterized by upland hardwoods and pine forests on the higher banks banded by a corridor of lowland trees such as cypress, black gum, birch, and willow near the water. The serpentine course of the waterway lends itself to many sandbars, and campsites are not difficult to find. The water is usually tannin-stained except in areas where agricultural runoff may cloud it to a tannish yellow. In fact, the word Ochlockonee comes from the Hitchiti Indian language and is said to mean *yellow river*.

Upper sections of the river are owned by individuals and paper companies and care should be taken in selecting campsites. The lower part of the Ochlockonee River flows through the Apalachicola National

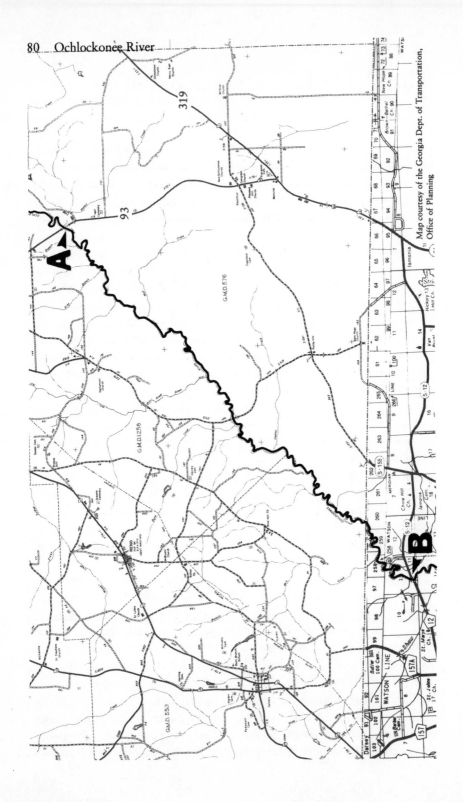

Map courtesy of the Georgia Dept. of Transportation, Office of Planning

Forest and there are a number of national forest recreational areas on its banks that provide good camping facilities. Most of these areas are located on the east bank off so-called lakes that are adjacent to the river and may be difficult to find. These lakes are actually arms or backwater areas of the river. A national forest map (available from the U.S. Forest Service, P.O. Box 1050, Tallahassee, FL 32302) will be invaluable to the paddler in locating these campsites. It is also wise to ask directions from fishermen about the location of specific sites.

Since most of the river is a part of various wildlife management areas, the variety of wildlife is extensive. Deer are commonly sighted as are raccoons, turtles, and alligators. Present, but less visible are black bears, wild hogs, and panthers. Endangered species found on the river are the Southern bald eagle and red-cockaded woodpecker. Fish are plentiful in the Ochlockonee and include bass, bream, and catfish.

Telogia Creek and the Little River are the two largest tributaries of the Ochlockonee. Telogia Creek, which was mentioned in the section on streams in the Apalachicola National Forest (page 77), flows into and through an extensive swamp and is not suitable for recreational canoeing. Little River is formed a few miles below the Georgia line by the confluence of Willacoochee Creek and Attapulgus Creek and flows for 12 miles to Lake Talquin. It is like a miniature version of the Ochlockonee and is a very pleasant run. It passes through property owned by large hunting clubs and access is limited. Some of the largest deer herds in the United States are found on this river, including a variety of rare albino deer. Limited access and the protection of the hunting clubs have also resulted in extensive bird and other wildlife population. Very large alligators have been sighted and every sandbar is a tracker's paradise.

Georgia State Road 93 to Florida State Road 12 (A–B): 15 miles

DIFFICULTY: Moderate
SCENERY: Good
COUNTIES: Grady (Georgia), Gadsden (Florida)

ACCESS: From Thomasville, Georgia, travel south on U.S. 319 to the intersection with S.R. 93. Turn right (north) on S.R. 93 and continue to the bridge across the Ochlockonee.

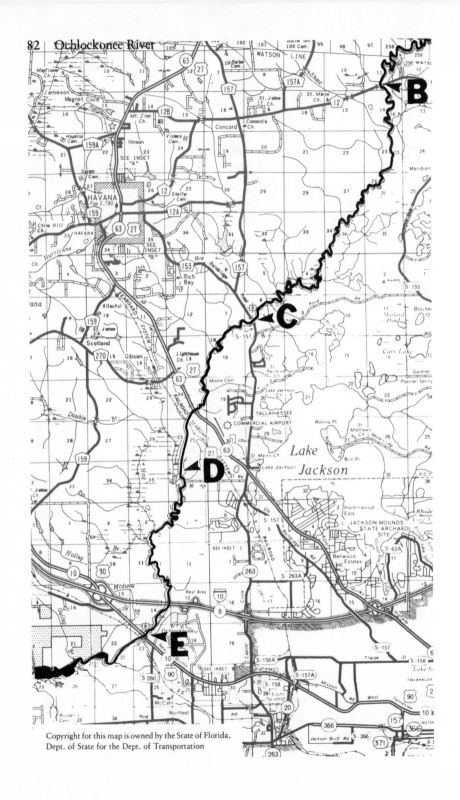

TRIP DESCRIPTION: Although adventurous canoeists sometimes put in above this point, this is generally considered the most northern section of the Ochlockonee that can be paddled with any degree of ease. Even so, it too should be avoided during periods of low water; in the summer months the overhanging branches of willow thickets can lead to an uncomfortable trip.

The stream tends to be very narrow and twisting with many obstructions such as stobs and downed trees in the waterway. Since it drains from a vast agricultural area, the water is usually a muddy brown. There are some sandbars on the insides of bends that can be used for campsites. The banks tend to be heavily forested and are usually private property.

Three miles below the put-in there is a county road that crosses the river and six miles downstream, there is an access from a graded road on the west bank.

Florida State Road 12 to State Road 157 (Old Bainbridge Road) (B–C): 14 miles

DIFFICULTY: Moderate
SCENERY: Good
COUNTY: Gadsden

ACCESS: From Tallahassee, travel north on U.S. 27 ten miles to the intersection with S.R. 157. Turn right (east) and continue across the bridge that crosses the Ochlockonee to the intersection with S.R. 12. Turn right (east) and continue to the river.

TRIP DESCRIPTION: This is a very remote section of river—the terrain tends to be swampy behind a corridor of banks and hardwoods. The current is generally slow and lazy, around large sweeping turns, making a long 14 miles. The water may still be yellowish in color, but is not as muddy as the upper sections since it is now draining a swampy area and is influenced by tannin-colored tributaries.

Four miles down from the put-in, the Ochlockonee flows within a mile of a large lake, Lake Iamonia, to the east. There is an extensive swamp between the river and the lake and at its south end, a number of small creeks flow in from the east bank. This is a section of river with a generous populations of alligators.

The river is crooked throughout and there are frequently sandbars on the bends. There are several fishing-hunting camps, but no signs of development. As one approaches the bridge at S.R. 157, fishermen in small boats may be encountered.

State Road 157 to Tower Road (C–D): 6 miles

DIFFICULTY: Moderate
SCENERY: Good
COUNTIES: Gadsden, Leon

ACCESS: From Tallahassee, travel north on U.S. 27 ten miles to the intersection with S.R. 157. Turn right (east) and continue to the bridge across the Ochlockonee. Access is on the northwest side of the bridge.

TRIP DESCRIPTION: Although the river has become wider and less winding, it still has many turns and the potential for a lot of obstacles. There is some evidence of development in this section. It is four miles to U.S. 27, a dual lane highway with no good access to the river. Below U.S. 27, the river runs very straight for two miles to just above the boat ramp at Tower road. Directly above the boat ramp the river makes an oxbow around a small island; the ramp is on the east bank.

Tower Road to U.S. 90 (D–E): 5 miles

DIFFICULTY: Easy
SCENERY: Good
COUNTIES: Leon, Gadsden

ACCESS: From Tallahassee, travel north for ten miles on U.S. 27. At the intersection with S.R. 157, turn left (west) and continue for less than one-half mile to the first graded road to the right (west), Tower road. Turn right and continue for less than two miles to the river. Access is from a public boat ramp.

TRIP DESCRIPTION: Below the Tower road landing, the river begins to engage in some extreme turns again, often almost doubling back on itself. The current is very slow and the banks begin to be low and swampy. After the first two miles below the put-in, the river becomes less twisting. It flows under Interstate 10 about one mile above the bridge across the Ochlockonee River.

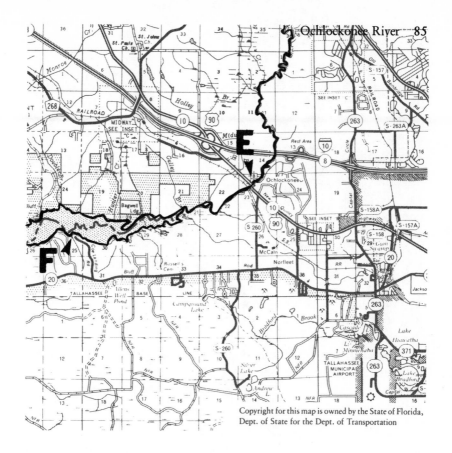

Copyright for this map is owned by the State of Florida,
Dept. of State for the Dept. of Transportation

U.S. 90 to Coes Landing (E–F): 6 miles

DIFFICULTY: Moderate
SCENERY: Excellent
COUNTY: Leon

ACCESS: From Tallahassee, travel west on U.S. 90 for eight miles to the bridge across the Ochlockonee River. Access is from a public boat ramp on the northwest side of the bridge.

TRIP DESCRIPTION: Below U.S. 90, the river becomes even wider and there is a mile long straight stretch. Banks along this stretch tend to be high and there are some houses on the east side for a short distance downstream. Once they are passed, the river becomes remote again. The west side of the river is owned by a private wildlife management group and there is virtually no access.

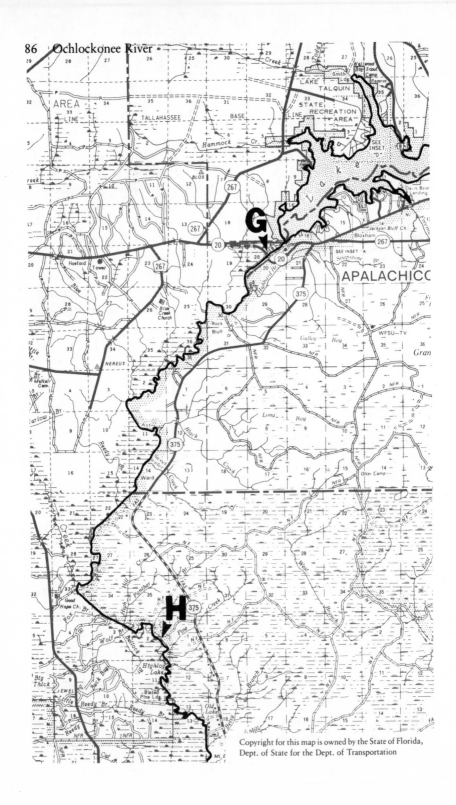

In the second mile, the river begins to wind again and it becomes swampier as it nears Lake Talquin. Bird life is abundant in this area and there are some fine stands of pine in the highlands east of the river. By the beginning of the third mile downstream, the river widens as the lake begins. Hammocks and islands dot the waterway and by the time Coes Landing is reached, the lake is more than one-half mile wide. At this point, wind and waves may become a problem for the canoeist. Coes Landing is located on the east bank and is easily seen from the lake.

Lake Talquin stretches for another 13 miles to the dam at S.R. 20 and becomes increasingly wide. It is also frequented by large motorboats. It is a beautiful lake and a worthwhile experience for those who enjoy lake paddling. At the end of the lake, Talquin Dam must be portaged.

State Road 20 to Pine Creek Landing (G–H): 15 miles

DIFFICULTY: Moderate
SCENERY: Excellent
COUNTIES: Leon, Liberty

ACCESS: From Tallahassee, travel west for 22 miles on S.R. 20 to the bridge across the Ochlockonee River. There is access on either side of the river from privately owned boat ramps. There is a fee for launching.

TRIP DESCRIPTION: The Ochlockonee is dam-controlled from this point to its terminus at Ochlockonee Bay, but usually water levels are consistent with the amount of rainfall received by the area during the previous week. To be on the safe side, information about water release can be obtained by calling (904) 576-8233.

The first mile below the put-in at S.R. 20 is a straight stretch of river 150 feet wide with a road down the east bank. There are fish camps and houses in this area; the Apalachicola National Forest boundaries begin at the end of the first bend in the river, and its remote characteristics resume. The west bank of the river is privately owned, primarily by a large paper company, and there is no access on that side for many miles. Small fishing boats are common on the lower stretches of the river, but they are seldom encountered more than two miles from a boat landing.

Two miles downstream from S.R. 20 is an access at Rock Bluff Scenic Area which is reached from F.R. 390. It is a high bluff on the

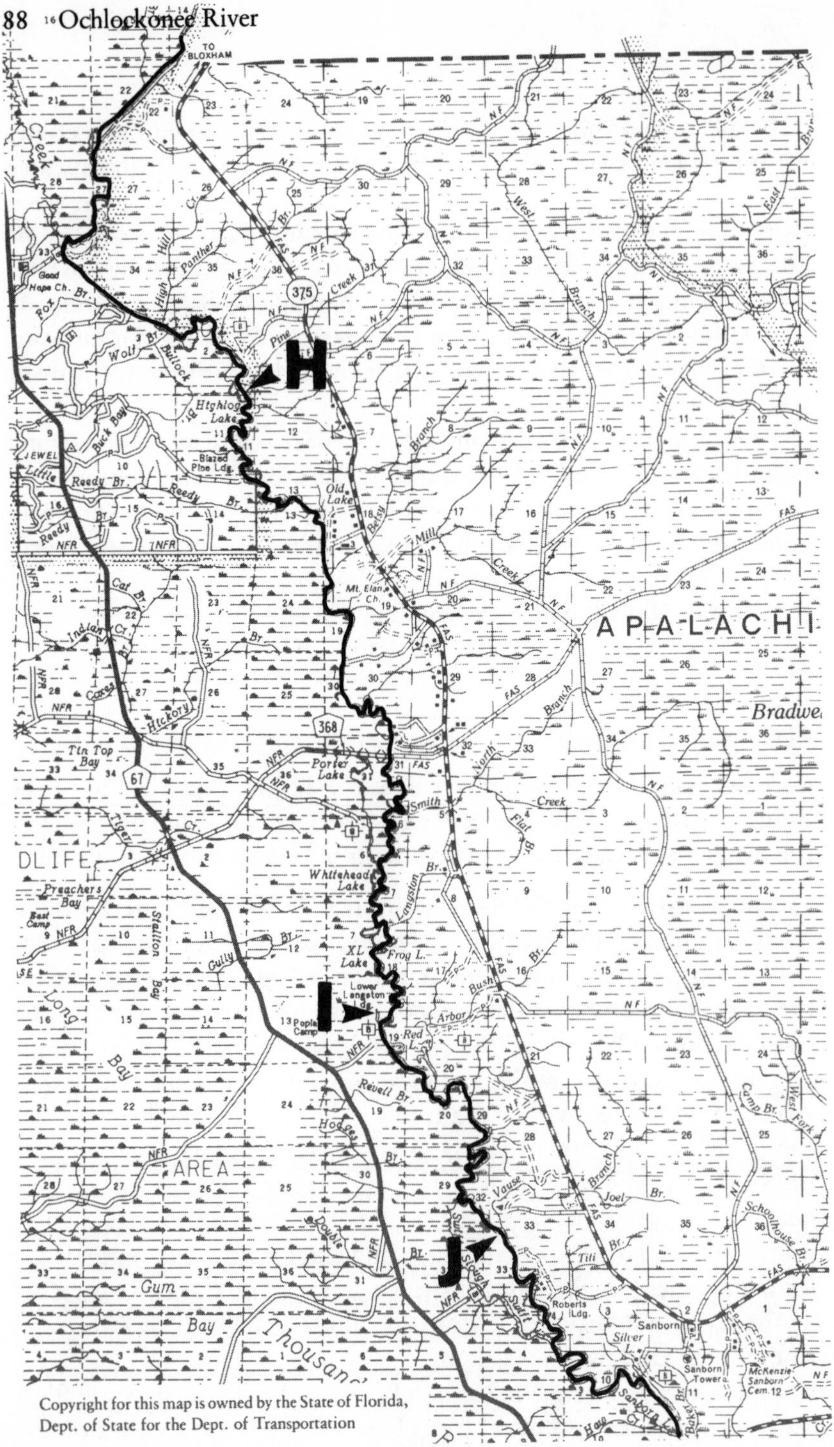
H
I
J
APALACHI
AREA
DLIFE
Bradwe
Highlog Lake
Blazed Pine Ldg.
Old Lake
Mt. Elon Ch.
Porter Lake
Whitehead Lake
XL Lake
Frog L.
Lower Langston Ldg.
Poplar Camp
Red L.
Roberts Ldg.
Sanborn
Silver L.
Sanborn Tower
McKenzie Sanborn Cem.
Good Hope Ch.
Tin Top Bay
Preachers Bay
Gum Bay
Long Bay
Thousand
TO BLOXHAM
375
368
67

east bank with good access to the river and a large grassy area suitable for camping.

The river alternates between long straight stretches and sharp bends. It tends to narrow in the curving sections and has a better current with sandbars on the insides of some of the bends. Three miles downstream from Rock Bluff is Stoutamire Landing, a privately owned boat launch, with some small cabins nearby. Drake Landing, also private, is two miles farther downstream with another high bluff on the east side of the river.

Telogia Creek flows into the Ochlockonee from the west bank 12 miles from S.R. 20. Here is a public boat ramp (reached from S.R. 67 in Liberty County) and a high bank with a group of houses. From this point, it is another three miles to Pine Creek Landing. This is a very popular area for hunting during the season from mid-November to mid-January. Use caution in selecting a campsite and do not take dogs or firearms on the river unless you camp on forest property and have the required licenses and permits.

Pine Creek Landing to Lower Langston Landing (H–I): 13 miles

DIFFICULTY: Moderate
SCENERY: Excellent
COUNTIES: Leon, Wakulla

ACCESS: From Tallahassee, travel west on S.R. 20 to the community of Bloxham (Leon County), and the junction with S.R. 375. Turn left (south) on S.R. 375 and continue for ten miles to the junction with F.R. 335, a graded road. Turn right (west) and continue for one and one-half miles to the river. Access is from a paved public boat ramp.

TRIP DESCRIPTION: The river is 150 feet wide at this point with low banks on the east side and a swampy area on the west. There is a high, grassy area around the boat launch that could be used for camping.

Soon after leaving Pine Creek, the river narrows again and in many spots is constricted by overhanging willow branches and downed trees. As a result, some degree of skill in maneuvering is needed. There are small sandbars scattered along in the bends of the river, but they are usually covered by willow trees and river birch and are not large enough to be good campsites. This is a heavily forested section and is remote except for one house on the west bank about halfway between Pine Creek and Upper Langston Landing.

Upper Langston, accessible from S.R. 375, is three miles downstream from Pine Creek on the east bank. It is privately owned; there is a fee for camping and launching. There is also a small store there and potable water.

Just before reaching this landing, the river divides and becomes very narrow and swift as it flows around a small island. It is usually best to stay to the west channel. The river widens at the end of the island.

From Upper Langston Landing to F.R. 13 is another four miles. This section is less remote with some houses scattered along the east bank. The bridge across the Ochlockonee at F.R. 13 is the first one to be encountered for 22 miles and the last one on the sections of the river covered in this guide. There is no access to the river from F.R. 13 which is unfortunate. Just west of this bridge, across two more bridges, is a nice campground at Porter Lake. This campground can be reached by paddling downstream from F.R. 13 for about two and one-half miles to the point where Porter Lake flows into the Ochlockonee and then paddling upstream to the campsite. There is no good way to identify this spot, since there are many lakes and sloughs on the west side of the river and an entire day could be spent paddling up each of them in search of the right one. These so-called lakes are actually arms or backwaters of the river.

Lower Langston Landing to Mack Landing (I–J): 6 miles

DIFFICULTY: Moderate
SCENERY: Excellent
COUNTIES: Liberty, Wakulla

ACCESS: From Tallahassee, travel west on S.R. 20 to the community of Bloxham, and the junction with S.R. 375. Turn left (south) on S.R. 375 and continue to the junction with F.R. 13, the first paved road that turns right (west). Turn right on F.R. 13 and cross the river and two additional bridges. Continue for about three miles to the intersection with S.R. 67. Turn left (south) on S.R. 67 and continue for another three miles to the junction with F.R. 152. Turn left (east) on F.R. 152 and continue for one mile to the river. Access is from a paved public boat ramp.

TRIP DESCRIPTION: Lower Langston Landing is located on a high, pleasant site on the west bank of the river. It is a good camping area but has no facilities. About one-quarter of a mile downstream from the landing, there is a large sandbar on the east bank at the point where a small creek flows into the river. This is also a pleasant campsite and is not accessible by road. At normal- to high-water levels, these are the last campsites until Mack Landing is reached. In this section, the river continues to alternate between wide, straight sections and narrow bends.

Mack Landing to Wood Lake (J–K): 12 miles

DIFFICULTY: Easy
SCENERY: Good
COUNTY: Wakulla, Liberty

ACCESS: From Tallahassee, travel west on S.R. 20 to the community of Bloxham and the junction with S.R. 375. Turn left (south) on S.R. 375 and continue to the junction with F.R. 336, a distance of 21 miles. There will be a sign indicating the Mack Landing Recreation Area. Turn right (west) on F.R. 336 and continue to the river. Access is from a paved public boat ramp.

TRIP DESCRIPTION: There is an established campground at Mack Landing with tables, grills, primitive toilets, and a pump with potable water. Unfortunately, like most of the other national forest access points, it is located off one of the many lakes on the east side of the river that are indistinguishable from one another. When attempting to find these landings from the river, the best strategy is to ask any fishermen that you may see.

Mack Landing can be distinguished because of the very high banks that begin to run along the east bank at this point. They are 10 to 12 feet high and look as if they have been cleared on top. They continue for one mile to the Roberts Landing area where there is a privately owned boat ramp and several houses.

Although the river continues to curve for the next three miles, the bends are much wider and more gentle than they have been previously. There is an access at Silver Lake, on the east bank, just at the end of this curving section, but it, too, is difficult to find.

The paddler then enters a two-mile-long straight section that is broad, frequented by large motorboats, and may be affected by wind and tide.

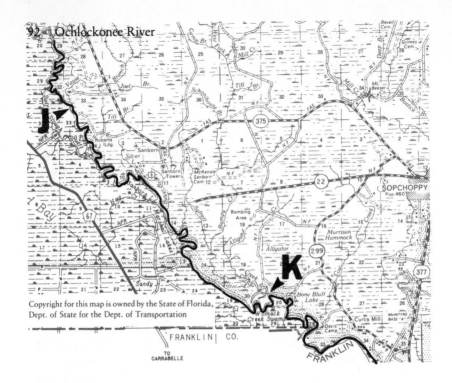

Copyright for this map is owned by the State of Florida,
Dept. of State for the Dept. of Transportation

There is another mile or so of a curving section and then another three-mile stretch on an increasingly large and populated river. The banks are heavily forested in this area with some high pinelands alternating with swamp. At high- to normal-water levels campsites are small and scarce. At the end of the three-mile stretch, there is a camp with a rough cabin on a bend on the east bank. A small, white sandbar extends to the south of it. At this point, one should begin to watch for the landing one mile downstream on the east bank of Wood Lake.

Those who wish to do so may paddle for another ten miles to the Ochlockonee River State Park. At that point the river is the size of a small bay and is frequented by water-skiers, large powerboats, and even sailboats. It is also heavily influenced by the tide. Most canoeists prefer to end their trip at Wood Lake.

TAKE-OUT (K): From Sopchoppy, travel west on S.R. 22 for one and a half miles to the intersection with S.R. 299. Turn left (south) on S.R. 299 and travel three miles to the junction with F.R. 338. Turn right (west) and continue toward the lake. There is a national forest recreation area campground at Wood Lake with tables, grills, primitive toilets, and a water pump.

Little River

The Little River, a tributary of the Ochlockonee, is formed a few miles above S.R. 12 by the convergence of Willacoochee and Attapulgus creeks. It flows into the Ochlockonee at Lake Talquin. It is possible to put in at S.R. 12, but the access is poor, and the upper section of the river is characterized by many pull-overs and shallow water in all but the wettest of seasons. Further, both sides of the riverbank are owned by private hunting clubs that not only discourage its usage, but make it somewhat hazardous during hunting season. This is also true of much of the lower section, but the river is wider, deeper, and easier to maneuver, making a pleasant trip for the spring and early fall.

U.S. 90 to State Road 268 (A–B): 4 miles

DIFFICULTY: Moderate
SCENERY: Excellent
COUNTY: Gadsden

ACCESS: From Tallahassee, travel west on U.S. 90 16 miles to the bridge across the Little River. Access is on the southeast side of the bridge.

TRIP DESCRIPTION: A considerable number of obstructions on this section of the river require some skill in maneuvering. There is usually a pleasant current and the banks are intermittent swampy areas interspersed with some 20-foot-high bluffs. Several sandbars would make adequate campsites. About three miles below U.S. 90, Interstate 10 crosses the river.

State Road 268 to High Bluff on Lake Talquin (B–C): 5 miles

DIFFICULTY: Moderate
SCENERY: Excellent
COUNTY: (Leon), Gadsden

ACCESS: From Tallahassee, travel west on U.S. 90 12 miles to the town of Midway, and the intersection with S.R. 268. Turn left (south) on S.R. 268 and continue for five miles to the bridge across the Little River.

TRIP DESCRIPTION: Below S.R. 268, the river widens and becomes both deeper and straighter. The sandbars disappear; the banks become high

93

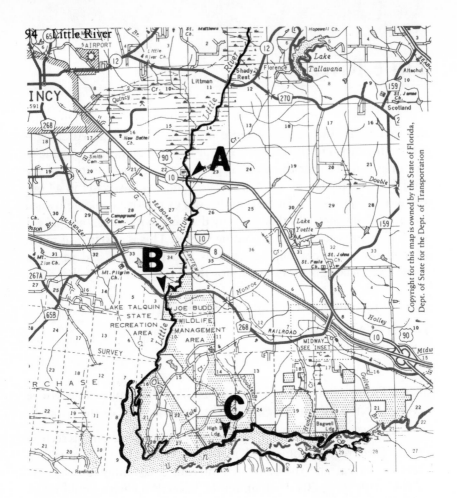

and heavily wooded. As the river nears Lake Talquin, it becomes swampier with small bayous and sloughs off to the sides. When it flows into the lake, the water becomes shallower with many stumps showing above the water. After entering the lake, the paddler should turn left, or north, and remain on the west side. This is the upper portion of Lake Talquin; it is wide and may be windy. It is three miles from the confluence of Little River up the lake to High Bluff.

TAKE-OUT (C): From Tallahassee, travel west on U.S. 90 12 miles to the town of Midway and the intersection with S.R. 268. Turn left (south) on S.R. 268 and continue for about three miles. Turn left (south) on a graded road. Stay to the left at all junctions and continue for three miles to High Bluff where there is a public boat ramp and a primitive camping area.

The St. Marks River Basin

The St. Marks River and its beautiful tributary, the Wakulla, are the most northern of the wide, clear, spring-fed rivers that are so much a part of the attraction of Florida waterways. A tiny, swamp-lined stream meandering from a series of ponds north of U.S. 90 is ambitiously named the St. Marks River, but it is not until the advent of the waters from Horn Spring that it becomes a canoeable stream. Then, just two and one-half miles later, it goes underground to form the famous Natural Bridge of historical repute. After flowing under the roadway, forming a true natural bridge, the river resumes again with St. Marks Spring and flows some eleven miles to its confluence with the Wakulla and three miles on to the Gulf of Mexico.

A small state historic memorial is located at the Natural Bridge on the St. Marks River. On this site, Confederate militia repulsed Federal forces on 6 March 1865 and prevented capture of Tallahassee, the only southern capital east of the Mississippi not captured in the Civil War.

The Wakulla is a large river from its origin at Wakulla Springs, billed as the World's Largest Spring. Indian Springs, Sally Ward Spring, and McBride Slough also contribute to the crystal waters of the Wakulla River. The property around the springhead is owned by a resort (but, as of this writing, is being purchased for a state park) and public access to the river is restricted to the S.R. 365 bridge. At Wakulla Springs, swimming, diving, and resort tour boats are available for a fee, but there are no provisions for canoe rental or for launching private boats.

Both the Wakulla and the St. Marks rivers flow through swampy terrain with a preponderance of cypress, magnolia, palm, and other lowland vegetation. They are clear, blue green rivers resulting from the limestone bottoms with a variety of water weeds above and below the surface. The current is mild on both rivers and it is possible to paddle upstream easily.

At the confluence of the two rivers, the state has built a replica of San Marcos de Apalache, a Spanish fort that occupied the site in 1718. Wooden stockades were built by the Spanish in 1680 and 1758, but were destroyed by hurricanes. A masonary fort was begun in 1759, but was abandoned to the Indians for a trading post. General Andrew Jackson seized the fort in 1819; it was occupied as an army post until 1824. Later, it was reestablished and occupied by the Confederate Army during the Civil War.

The St. Marks River

Horn Spring to Natural Bridge (A–B): 2.5 miles

DIFFICULTY: Easy
SCENERY: Excellent
COUNTY: Leon

ACCESS: From Woodville, travel east on S.R. 260 (Natural Bridge road) to the Natural Bridge and the wooden bridge to the second dirt trail to the left. Turn left and continue two miles to the spring. This is a rough, unmaintained road and may have deep sand and/or bog holes.

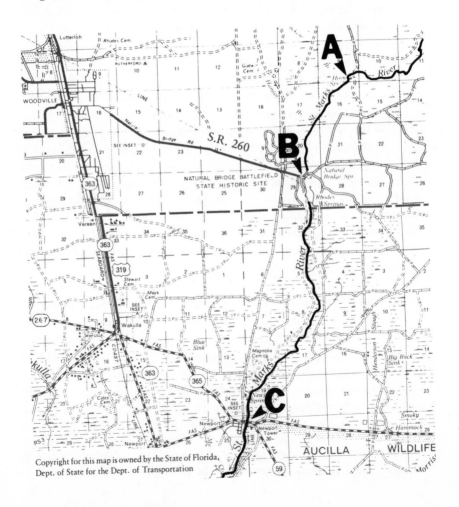

Copyright for this map is owned by the State of Florida, Dept. of State for the Dept. of Transportation

TRIP DESCRIPTION: Although this section of the St. Marks River is short and often difficult to reach, it is of interest because of the deep hardwood forest, swampy terrain, and unusually large cypress trees present along the banks. It is possible to paddle upstream from the Natural Bridge as well and it is a pleasant afternoon conoeing experience in a pocket wilderness.

Horn Spring actually consists of two springs. The larger is 75 feet in diameter and 30 feet deep. When the sediment is undisturbed, it is a clear, green color. The smaller spring, 200 feet north, is only 30 feet in diameter. The two join to flow about 350 feet downstream into the St. Marks River.

Shortly below the influx of the spring runs, Chicken Branch enters the river from the west. Myriad unnamed seeping springs and small creeks lace the swamps beside the river. A number of very large cypress trees still stand in this area as well as magnolias, palms, and other typical lowland vegetation.

This section of the St. Marks River goes underground at the Natural Bridge. There are several springs in the area of the Natural Bridge that are probably reoccurrences of the river. These include Natural Bridge Spring and at least four springs in the Rhodes Springs group. They rise in an area that has a dense growth of vegetation, swamp, and karst features such as sinkholes and solution tubes. The river does not rise as a well-defined riverbed until about three-quarters of a mile south of S.R. 260 at St. Marks Springs.

St. Marks Springs to Newport Bridge (U.S. 98) (C): 12 miles round trip to St. Marks Springs

DIFFICULTY: Easy
SCENERY: Good
COUNTIES: Leon, Wakulla

ACCESS: Unfortunately, the property south of Natural Bridge road (S.R. 260), is privately owned and there is no public access to St. Marks Spring or the rise of the St. Marks River. It is possible to paddle upstream from the Newport Bridge (U.S. 98), however, a distance of about 12 miles round trip.

TRIP DESCRIPTION: The river from St. Marks Spring to Newport Bridge is wide and has lively current near the headspring but becomes narrower and slower within the first mile. It is a very clear and beautiful waterway with intermittent swamp and highland banks. About one mile above Newport, the run from Newport Spring, formerly called Brewer Sulphur Spring, enters from the west bank. It is characterized by its highly pungent odor of sulphur.

The confluence of the St. Marks with the Wakulla River is five miles below the Newport Bridge. A very old boat works, houses, commercial establishments, and a marina are on this section. It is also used as a harbor for fishing boats and other marine craft. It is generally not of interest to a canoeist.

The Wakulla River

The primary source of the Wakulla River is Wakulla Springs. Said to be the largest spring in Florida and perhaps in the world, it is the site of a 1920s hotel and resort. Wildlife, especially birds and alligators, are a major attraction. The unusual clarity of the spring water has resulted in its being chosen for a number of motion pictures over the years. Despite lengthy legal proceedings, the owners of the resort have been permitted to maintain a fence across the river just above S.R. 365 that prevents access to the first three miles of this navigable-to-canoes stream. Paddling a canoe under the fence is obviously easy to do but should be strongly discouraged as this is a very sensitive issue with the property owners.

State Road 365 to U.S. 98 (A–B): 4 miles

DIFFICULTY: Easy
SCENERY: Good
COUNTY: Wakulla

ACCESS: From Tallahassee, travel south on S.R. 363 to the intersection of S.R. 267. Turn west (right), and then turn left at the fork onto S.R. 365. Continue two miles to the bridge across the river.

TRIP DESCRIPTION: It is possible to canoe both up and downstream on this section, eliminating the need for a shuttle. The current is gentle, the river is broad, clear, and very beautiful. There are several islands, but generally they can be run on either side.

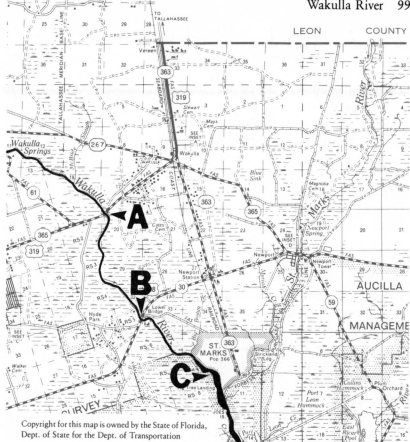

U.S. 98 to St. Marks City Park (B–C): 2 miles

DIFFICULTY: Easy
SCENERY: Good
COUNTY: Wakulla

ACCESS: From Tallahassee, travel south on S.R. 363 to the intersection with U.S. 98. Turn right (west) and continue to the bridge.

TAKE-OUT (C): From the city of St. Marks, follow the plainly marked street that goes west toward Fort San Marcos de Apalache. The fort road will junction, with traffic to the left going to the fort, and traffic to the right going to the city park. To take out at the city park, turn right and continue until the park is seen on the left.

The Aucilla and Wacissa Rivers

The Aucilla and Wacissa, perhaps the most popular canoeing rivers in Florida's Big Bend area, are only a few miles apart, but are totally different. There is some evidence that the Wacissa is a tributary of the Aucilla, but both of them have such strange and unruly habits that it is difficult to document this relationship. The Aucilla begins just south of Boston, Georgia, and flows into the Gulf of Mexico south of the confluence of the St. Marks. It pops up and down with such irregularity, however, that in many places it is not a river at all but a series of lakes, marshes, and/or sinkholes. Just north of U.S. 27, the Aucilla makes up into a clearly defined river and proceeds in an orderly fashion for about twenty miles until it goes underground again. It rises some five miles to the south and is joined by the waters of the Wacissa, flowing through a man-made canal on to the Gulf.

The Aucilla, limestone ringed and bedded with dark, clear tannin water and beautiful vegetation, varies from high banks with upland hardwoods to more tropical-looking areas of cypress, palms, and palmettos. The reflections of the trees in the dark water is a treat at any season of the year. There are two relics of man-made dams on the upper section that may provide an easy whitewater experience for the novice paddler. Since the dams were built of native limestone that has now washed aside, there are no dangerous hydraulics or undercurrents. On the lower section, there are a series of rocky shoals, and at the point where the Tallahassee hills drop off the karst, a stretch of real whitewater appears. Dropping eight to ten feet over 30 yards of boulder-strewn river, the Big Rapid is about the best Florida has to offer the whitewater buff. A few more miles through increasingly beautiful jungle-like terrain, and the Aucilla goes underground. No dramatics— just a quiet pool with a few logs floating around.

Ten miles west of the Aucilla, the Wacissa River, fed by 12 first magnitude springs, rises broad and crystal clear. The area adjoining the river is densely forested with cypress, oak, and pine and is generally so swampy that access to most of the springs is only available by boat. The river is very broad and flat for the first five miles below the headsprings with numerous water weeds and swampy banks. An island, about three miles down, is the first high ground. There is also high ground five miles down at Wacissa Dam, built for a narrow-gage railroad that once crossed the river at this point. Below the dam the river narrows and runs around islands and off into swift, narrow fingers. Less than two miles above a recreation area, Goose Pasture, the river again broadens and continues past the recreation area for another half mile. This is not truly the river, however, and the water soon begins to run off into the Western Sloughs that lead into an unnavigable swamp called Hell's Half Acre.

The real Wacissa flows to the extreme west opposite Goose Pasture, and eventually into the Slave Canal. This canal was built shortly after 1831 by the Wacissa and Aucilla Navigation Company and connected the Wacissa River with the Aucilla River, thus providing a waterway to the Gulf of Mexico for the transport of cotton from the Jefferson County plantations. The canal provides a beautiful, eerie, and unusual canoeing experience on clear, shallow water through deep swamp. The two rivers join just above U.S. 98 and the Aucilla, having just popped up again at Nutal Rise, continues to the Gulf.

The five remaining miles of river, from U.S. 98 to the Gulf is bounded on one side by the St. Marks National Wildlife Refuge and on the other by property owned by a large paper company. There is not a good access to the river; most canoeists end their trip at U.S. 98.

The Wacissa River

Wacissa to Goose Pasture (A–B): 9 miles

DIFFICULTY: Easy
SCENERY: Excellent
COUNTY: Jefferson

ACCESS: From Tallahassee, travel east on U.S. 27 to S.R. 59. Turn right (south) and continue to the town of Wacissa. When S.R. 59 turns west, continue straight ahead for a quarter mile to the river. There is a recreation area with a diving board and boat launch.

TRIP DESCRIPTION: Many canoeists do not go downriver on the Wacissa, but spend a pleasant day or afternoon paddling around the springs' area. The 12 named springs are scattered along the upper two miles of the river. Big Blue Spring, about one mile downriver on the east bank is one of the most popular of the group. The pool is 120 feet in

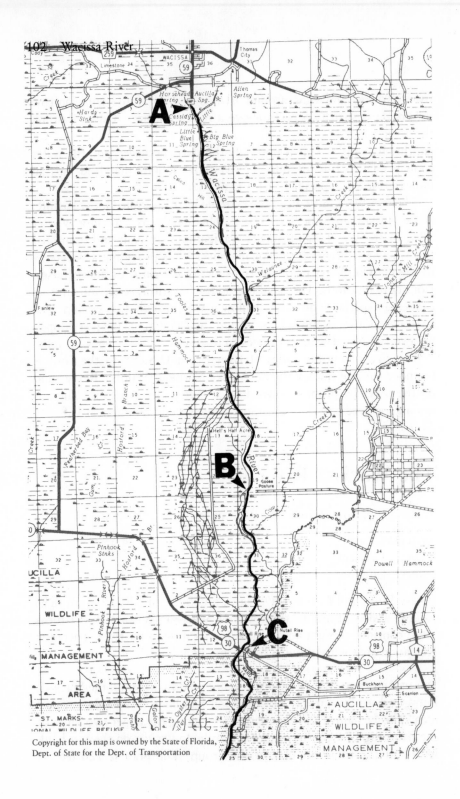

diameter and 45 feet deep over the vent. The limestone bottom is cavernous and the spring flows from several ledges on the northwest side of the vent.

Cedar Island is three miles below the headspring and marks the end of the spring area. Paddlers who plan to paddle back upstream to Wacissa probably should not progress beyond this point. There is a small cleared area on the island, good for lunch breaks and possible overnight camping for one or two tents.

The Wacissa Dam, the site of an old narrow-gauge railroad, offers a swift chute that poses no hazard for the canoeist. There are some buildings just below here on the west bank, that are on private property. Shortly below the dam, the Wacissa narrows and becomes interspersed with a number of low islands and hammocks which divide the river into small channels. This area is not large and if one chooses the wrong way, it is a simple matter to back up and start over. Just over a mile above Goose Pasture the river widens again into a long grassy area. For a mile above this grassy area the river is canopied, swift, and may have some downed trees to pull over.

Goose Pasture through the Slave Canal to the Aucilla River at U.S. 98 (B–C): 5 miles

DIFFICULTY: Easy
SCENERY: Superb
COUNTIES: Jefferson, Taylor

ACCESS: Although there are two or three points where the Wacissa can be reached by road between Wacissa and Goose Pasture, these roads are remote, unmarked, and in unreliable condition. The road into Goose Pasture is usually bumpy and poorly maintained, but has the advantage of being well-traveled and easy to find.

When leaving the boat launch at Wacissa, return to S.R. 59 and follow it west-southwest to its intersection with U.S. 98, a distance of about 14 miles. At U.S. 98, turn left (east), crossing the Aucilla River bridge. After crossing the bridge, continue to the third dirt road to your left (about two miles). Turn left and continue on this broad, graded, limestone road for four miles to an intersection with another graded road. Turn left and continue to the Goose Pasture Recreation Area.

The Goose Pasture Recreation Area is an unsupervised camping and picnicking facility provided by the Buckeye Cellulous Corporation. It is closed to overnight camping during the hunting season. It is an extremely popular spot and not recommended for those desiring peace and quiet.

TRIP DESCRIPTION: When leaving Goose Pasture, paddle to the extreme west side of the river. Follow the current through the stands of wild rice down a narrow waterway and through a swampy area for about one-half mile. A clearly defined channel 25 to 30 feet wide will emerge. Continue on this channel for about one mile. Begin watching for some very large cypress trees spaced along the left bank as the river widens. There will be a couple of small sloughs on the right side, but keep paddling and watch for a metal post. This post is to the right of the center of the stream. When you reach the post, watch carefully for a small opening due right of the post. Depending on the time of year and the abundance of vegetation, this channel may or may not be clear. Follow this channel and the flow of the water 25 yards and it will lead to a clear, well-defined canal, Slave Canal, through a beautiful swamp. If you fail to find the canal, return to the post and start over.

The Wacissa River wanders off into a large impassable swamp just south of the Slave Canal. Spending the night there makes a good story but can be a frightening and uncomfortable experience.

Once in the canal, the paddler enjoys a unique and eerie experience. This is a beautiful, clear, and shallow waterway through dense swamp. Magnificent cypress trees and other impressive hardwoods canopy the stream and it is a rare day when the paddler doesn't see alligators, turtles, and a vast variety of waterbirds. It is awe inspiring to consider that human labor is responsible for what now appears to be a natural waterway.

At the end of the canal, the canoeist should paddle upstream for a few hundred yards to the boat landing on the Aucilla River. The point where the two streams meet is easily recognized as a strong current flows past the Slave Canal from the east.

TAKE-OUT (C): From the town of Newport, travel east on U.S. 98 for 15 miles to the bridge across the Aucilla River. After crossing the river, turn left on the first graded road—this leads to a boat launch area.

The Aucilla River

From U.S. 27 to State Road 257 (A–B): 13 miles

DIFFICULTY: Easy to Moderate
SCENERY: Excellent
COUNTIES: Madison, Jefferson

ACCESS: From Tallahassee, travel east on U.S. 27 for 29 miles to the town of Lamont. Just southeast of Lamont a bridge crosses the Aucilla River.

TRIP DESCRIPTION: While it is possible to paddle on the Aucilla for several miles upstream of this point, the stream is small and frequently obstructed. There are also some rocky shoals that would require either lifting over or a portage. Most canoeists prefer to go downriver from U.S. 27. About one mile below the put-in are the remains of the first of two man-made dams. These dams were constructed of native limestone and have been washed away, resulting in nice little drops or rapids. Since they were not excavated or reinforced in any way, they do not have dangerous hydraulics or pieces of metal in them. Novice canoeists usually navigate them without difficulty, but if in doubt, they can easily be carried around.

This section of the river is primarily of the drop-and-pool nature with stretches of slow water broken by rocky shoals and small drops. The high banks have typical hardwood forests; some swampy areas provide a contrast of cypress, magnolia, and titi. Camping areas are plentiful in the woods and since most of this area is owned by a large paper company, it is open for recreational use. Care with open fires and litter will ensure that this policy remains in effect in the future.

From State Road 257 to Logging Road (B–C): 6 miles

DIFFICULTY: Moderate
SCENERY: Excellent
COUNTIES: Jefferson, Taylor

ACCESS: From Tallahassee, travel east on U.S. 27 for 29 miles to the town of Lamont. Turn south (right) on S.R. 257 and continue for seven miles to the bridge across the Aucilla River.

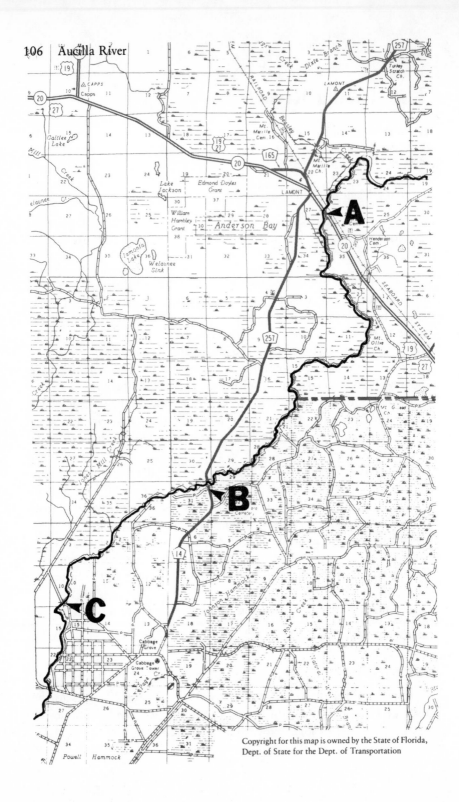

TRIP DESCRIPTION: There is usually a pleasant current on this section except in very low water. The banks are high and densely wooded with limestone outcroppings. Palm trees and the preponderance of resurrection fern on banks and oak limbs provide greenery even in the midst of winter.

The first set of rapids is encountered about two miles downstream. It is distinguished by a small, rocky shoal followed by a sharp bend to the right. The current speeds up and a sharp turn back to the left results in a shoal of cascading water for about 40 yards. It is a fairly easy run and poses little hazard to the reasonably competent canoeist.

Jones Mill Creek entering from the west indicates that the paddler is over halfway to the take-out. The creek usually spills over a limestone ledge when it enters the river and provides a pleasant swimming hole. The banks have been cleared here and it is a nice spot for camping and picnicking.

Less than a mile from Jones Mill Creek, the canoeist approaches the Big Rapid. This is a boulder–strewn drop of eight to ten feet over a distance of about 30 yards. It is true white-water, and should be accorded proper respect. The sound of fast water will usually be heard well in advance of the rapids and a quiet pool at the top makes it easy to pull over for scouting. Scout from the east bank where a well-worn trail runs beside the river. At very high water it may be impossible to tell that the rapid exists. At a reasonably high level, it may be run either on the right or left. Under normal conditions, it is run only on the left, or east side, of the river. Large logs and trees have been known to get caught in the rocks at the bottom of the rapid. This makes it essential that it be scouted prior to running.

There are several interesting shoals between the rapid and the take-out point, a distance of about one mile.

The river continues downstream from the take-out for about two miles before going underground. Access to this point is difficult and at most water levels will involve carrying canoes for several hundred yards over an eroded limestone trail. The river rises again at Nutal Rise and, with the confluence of the Slave Canal from the Wacissa just above U.S. 98, flows to the Gulf of Mexico. Access below U.S. 98 is limited.

TAKE-OUT (C): From the town of Lamont, travel south on S.R. 257 for seven miles to the bridge across the Aucilla River. Continue across the bridge on S.R. 257. After the pavement ends, continue south on the graded road for one-half mile, almost to the Cabbage Grove fire tower. Turn right on the first broad, graded road and proceed for just under one mile around the first bend to the left. Turn right on a smaller graded road, the logging road, and continue to an abandoned bridge. Just before reaching the bridge, a small trail to the right leads to a launching area on the river.

Other Coastal Rivers

The motorist traveling on U.S. 98 east of Newport and south of Perry, will cross several small rivers that are flowing to the Gulf of Mexico. Among them are the Econfina, Fenholloway, and Waccasassa rivers.

The Econfina River in Taylor County is a clear, unspoiled little stream with a jungle-like terrain. A four-mile run from U.S. 98 to an access off S.R. 14 makes a pleasant two-hour trip. Below that point, access is limited.

The Fenholloway River meanders for miles through Taylor County and is fed by ten named springs. Unfortunately, it has been so severly polluted by effluent from a paper mill that for years no vegetation or animal life grew in or near it. In addition, it gave off a most unpleasant odor. Recent environmental regulations have resulted in a clean-up project but it will be several years before this river is appropriate for recreational use again.

The Waccasassa River in Levy County near Gulf Hammock is a very wild and remote river with an abundance of animal and bird life. It is a fine example of coastal swamp and saw grass flats and is highly affected by the tide.

There is a six-mile trip from Gulf Hammock to the Gulf that is organized several times each year by the Game and Freshwater Fish Commission. Reservations are required and may be obtained through the Florida Department of Natural Resources.

The Northern Peninsula

Spring on the east side of Suwannee River,
two miles north of U.S. 90

Photograph by John Pearce

Withlacoochee River (North)

There are two rivers in Florida named Withlacoochee, the southern one is said to have been named after the one in the north. The northern Withlacoochee is really a Georgia river making up northwest of Valdosta and flowing some 70 miles through the coastal plain to the Florida line. It is said to be canoeable from Georgia S.R. 37 to the Suwannee River during periods of good rainfall and to be easily navigable from the confluence of Little River to the Suwannee at any time. From Florida S.R. 145 to Suwannee River State Park near U.S. 90 is a distance of about 36 miles.

The terrain on the Withlacoochee is similar to that of the upper Suwannee, characterized by high, limestone banks, clear black water, and an abundance of cypress and tupelo trees. There are also a number of small shoals in the river that serve to make the trip interesting but not dangerous. Blue Springs, a beautiful blue green pool, empties into the Withlacoochee from the west bank just a few yards from S.R. 6. This spring served as a major source of fresh water for the early inhabitants of the area. Another spring, Suwanacoochee, is located on the west side of the river just above Suwannee River State Park. At one time it served as the water supply for a public swimming pool whose remains are visible beside the river.

Campsites are not common on the Withlacoochee because of the steepness of the banks and the scarcity of sandbars. Upland hardwoods such as birch, water oak, redbud, magnolia, live oak, and pines are commonly seem. In the lower areas, cypress, tupelo, and other swamp trees are present. The remoteness of the river lends itself to an active bird life. The steep bank makes it difficult to sight wildlife but the forests of this area are known to harbor black bear, raccoon, opossum, wild boar, and bobcat.

The rocky shoals are discouraging to large boats, but fishermen in smaller johnboats are seen trying their luck at catfishing as well as angling for bream, bass, and trout.

State Road 145 to State Road 150 (A–B): 4 miles

DIFFICULTY: Easy
SCENERY: Good
COUNTY: Madison

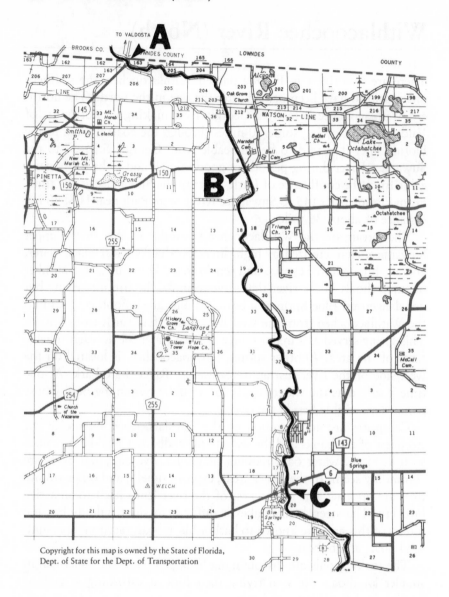

Copyright for this map is owned by the State of Florida,
Dept. of State for the Dept. of Transportation

ACCESS: From the town of Madison, travel northeast on S.R. 145 for about 18 miles to the bridge across the Withlacoochee. This will be just inside the Georgia line.

TRIP DESCRIPTION: The river is about 125 feet wide at this point and usually has a good current. A few small shoals wil be encountered.

State Road 150 to State Road 6 (B–C): 16 miles

DIFFICULTY: Easy
SCENERY: Good
COUNTY: Madison

ACCESS: From the town of Madison, travel northeast for 12 miles to Pinetta. Turn right (east) on S.R. 150 and continue to the river. The bridge is no longer in use.

TRIP DESCRIPTION: This is similar to Section A–B with some houses and camps scattered along the river banks. Some ten miles downriver from S.R. 150, there is a 10- to 12-foot opening in the high banks on the east side where water is rushing out of the river. If followed, this stream flows for 75 to 100 yards and disappears under a high bank. In Florida, whole rivers disappear in this manner, but it is unusual to lose just part of a river.

State Road 6 to Suwannee River State Park (C–D): 12 miles

DIFFICULTY: Easy
SCENERY: Good
COUNTIES: Madison, Hamilton

ACCESS: From the town of Madison, travel east on S.R. 6 for ten miles to the Withlacoochee.

TRIP DESCRIPTION: Just below the put-in on S.R. 6, Blue Springs flows in from the west bank. This is a very popular picnic and camping spot and on warm weekends will be crowded. The pool is 25 feet across with a single vent opening from a horizontal cavity 25 feet deep. The bottom is limestone and sand and there is a 25 foot high limestone bank on the south side. The current is milder below S.R. 6; the shoals become less frequent. The banks become increasingly higher and the limestone makes large white columns in fascinating shapes and forms. There are a number of unnamed springs along the banks in this section.

Just over a mile above the confluence with the Suwannee, S.R. 141 crosses the river, but there is no access to the water from this bridge. Suwanacoochee Spring, enclosed by a concrete wall, will be seen on the right. This spring pool is 20 feet in diameter with the water emerging from under a limestone ledge. The limestone outcrops around the

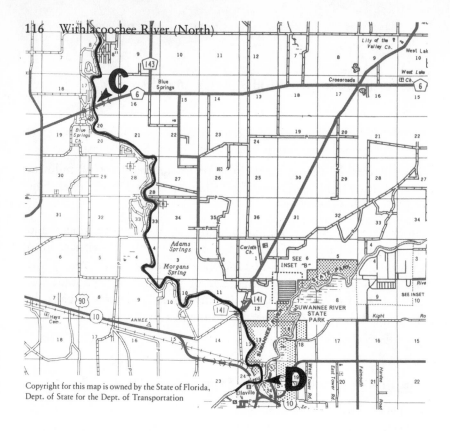

Copyright for this map is owned by the State of Florida,
Dept. of State for the Dept. of Transportation

pool are covered with green algae which presents a cool and appealing spot on a warm day.

After reaching the Suwannee, the paddler must turn north and paddle upstream for a short distance to the boat ramp. Keep in mind that state parks close at sundown. The ranger should be informed of your trip plans and will give you the combination to the gate should you arrive late. Another option is to paddle downstream a few yards to U.S. 90. There is a wayside park with picnic tables but no boat ramp and access from the water is poor.

TAKE-OUT (D): From the town of Madison, travel 17 miles east on U.S. 90 to the bridge across the Suwannee River. Cross the river and continue to the first road to the left. This is the entrance to Suwanee River State Park.

The Suwannee River

The Suwannee River is Florida's contribution to the Great Rivers of the world. While it would not win any prizes for grandiose size, spectacular canyons, or mighty ports, it is one of the South's last examples of "Old Man River." The name, Suwannee, is a very ancient Indian word that may have meant *echo*. Spelled a variety of ways, it appears in place names throughout the southeastern United States and has come to be synonymous with Dixie and the Old South. There are paddlers who have made the Suwannee their entire canoeing career. They need no other stream and never seek one.

The Suwannee drains out of the equally famous Okefenokee Swamp. A twisting river from its beginning just above Fargo, Georgia, it loops and curves across the Florida peninsula for over two hundred miles before it empties into the Gulf of Mexico. The upper stretches are characterized by sandy banks, rocky shoals, and a profusion of small waterfalls created by the entry of tiny streams. There are frequent swampy areas that provide overflow basins for flood waters. Stately cypress and gnarled tupelos often grow in the river as well as along the banks. Access is limited and the wildlife is abundant. Only the Withlacoochee River (north), the Alapaha River, and a few creeks feed the upper reaches of the Suwannee. As a result, the current tends to be slow and lazy except around the shoal areas. At low water, it is so undisturbed by current that it resembles a long, smooth lake mirroring white limestone banks and moss-draped trees.

A few miles above White Springs, a unique geological phenomenon produces Big Shoals, the largest whitewater shoal in Florida; it can be a strenuous rapid. Immediately below Big Shoals are a couple of small springs, harbingers of the fantastic array of springs that will be presented on the way to the Gulf. There are 22 major springs on the Suwannee and 27 on its tributary, the Santa Fe River. This accounts for the increasing size and volume of the river as it flows southward.

As in all rivers, the personality of the Suwannee undergoes a drastic change with the changes in water level. High water offers a faster current and easier paddling and makes Big Shoals a torrent of foaming, frothing turbulence. Low water is slower and more leisurely, but reveals white sandbars, gleaming castle-like limestone walls, and a treasure house of springs, caves, and grottos. In general, the Suwannee is high during the late winter and spring and becomes lower during the summer

117

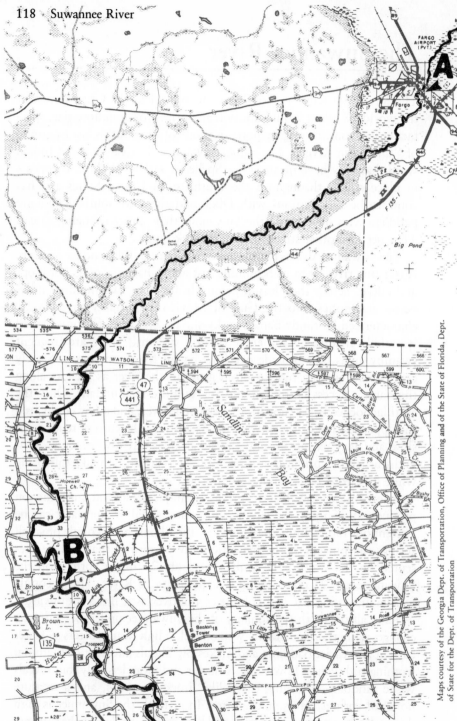

Maps courtesy of the Georgia Dept. of Transportation, Office of Planning and of the State of Florida, Dept. of State for the Dept. of Transportation

and fall. Autumn has the advantage of low water, pleasant weather, fewer bugs, and the beautiful fall colors reflected in the clear water.

Almost every tree indigenous to north Florida can be seen at some point on the Suwannee. Stands of cypress and yellow pine, gum, magnolia, maple, holly, poplar, willow, and river birch are common. Wildlife includes deer, otters, and alligators as well as beavers, raccoons, skunks, and armadillos.

Below Suwannee River State Park, the river broadens and becomes more accessible. This results in more motorboat traffic; the nearer the river gets to the Gulf, the larger and more powerful the boats that are encountered. Thus, even though the really spectacular springs are located in the coastal plain below U.S. 90, most canoeists prefer to end their trip there. For those who wish to paddle the lower sections, a summary of landmarks and access points will be included. The Suwannee River is easy, leisurely paddling for even a novice canoeist. Big Shoals can be easily scouted and portaged if necessary and none of the other shoals are sufficiently challenging to cause a problem. Roads run within a few miles of the river from Fargo, Georgia, to the Gulf and the countryside is dotted with crossroad communities and small towns.

Campsites are not plentiful on the Suwannee but every year hundreds of canoe-campers manage to find a spot to pitch a tent. Start looking well before sundown and be willing to compromise, something will turn up and once you have settled in, it will seem like home.

Fargo, Georgia, to Florida State Road 6 (A–B): 21 miles

DIFFICULTY: Easy
SCENERY: Excellent
COUNTIES: Clinch, Echols (GA), Hamilton (FL)

ACCESS: Fargo, Georgia, is located five miles north of the Florida-Georgia line at the intersection of U.S. 441 and Georgia S.R. 94. It is 38 miles due north of Lake City, Florida. The access is on the northeast side of the river. There is a paved boat ramp and a large, flat sandy area that could be used for camping.

TRIP DESCRIPTION: At this point, the Suwannee River has progressed 17 miles from Billys Lake in the Okefenokee Swamp and is 60 to 70 feet wide at low water. The banks are two to five feet high, sandy, and

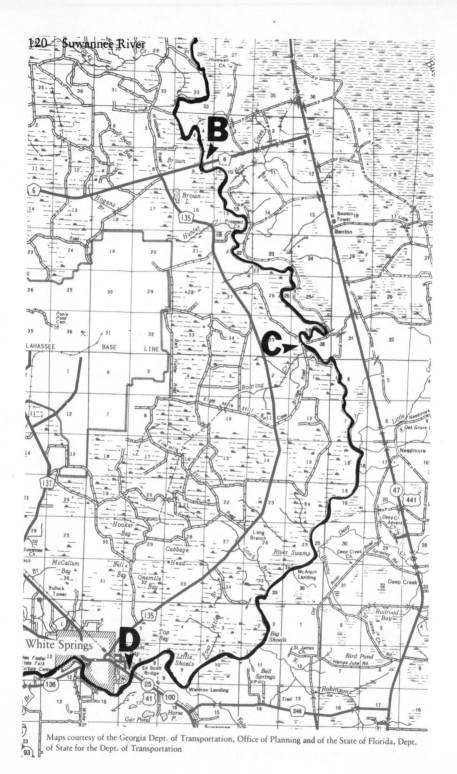

Maps courtesy of the Georgia Dept. of Transportation, Office of Planning and of the State of Florida, Dept. of State for the Dept. of Transportation

interspersed with large, swampy overflow areas. Campsites are scarce in high water but some small sandbars are available when the river is low. The current is usually slow to nonexistent so pace yourself accordingly. Cypress Creek enters from the east and Suwanoochee Creek from the west on this section. Woodpecker road, a graded and fairly well-maintained throughway, runs parallel to the river on the west. An access 15 miles south of Fargo can be reached from this road. There is a small shoal just above the S.R. 6 bridge.

State Road 6 to Cone Bridge Road (B–C): 10 miles

DIFFICULTY: Easy
SCENERY: Good
COUNTY: Hamilton

ACCESS: From White Springs, travel north on S.R. 135 for 17 miles to the intersection of S.R. 6. Turn right (east) and proceed to the bridge. The access is on the northwest side of the bridge; it is steep and in poor condition.

TRIP DESCRIPTION: There are a few houses and trailers for the first half mile or so below S.R. 6, but the wilderness soon returns. The banks have begun to be steeper since crossing the Florida line and this trend continues, making good campsites hard to find. Limestone outcroppings are more common and are frequently covered by bright green ferns which reflect in the still water. Tupelo and cypress growing in the water often form a line down each side of the river with hardwoods and pines growing above them on the steep banks. The effect of this natural corridor is serenely beautiful. This is an area of abundant wildlife; otters and alligators are a frequent sight for the quiet canoeist.

The waters of the upper Suwannee are extremely dark due to the tannin from the swamp. This tends to reduce the amount of fish life in this section but bass, catfish, and bream are caught.

S.R. 135 parallels the river on the west and a graded road is very near for most of the way on the east. There is an access four miles south of S.R. 6 at the end of Prospect Church road which turns east off S.R. 135. Metal pilings are the only remains of a bridge at Cone Bridge Road. There is a good public boat ramp and a grassy slope where camping would be possible. This access is often used by canoeists who wish to paddle down to Big Shoals.

Cone Bridge road to U.S. 41 (C–D): 15 miles

DIFFICULTY: Easy to Strenuous
SCENERY: Excellent
COUNTIES: Columbia, Hamilton

ACCESS: From the bridge on S.R. 6, travel east two miles to the inter-section with U.S. 441. Turn south on U.S. 441 and continue for approximately five miles. Cone Bridge road is on the right (west). Follow it for less than two miles to the river.

TRIP DESCRIPTION: The high banks and slow water continue and the lack of access makes this one of the most beautiful and remote sections of the river. Roaring Creek enters the river from the west just below Cone Bridge Road.

Deep Creek, a canoeable stream, flows in from the east about three miles above Big Shoals. Those wishing to paddle down Deep Creek should put in on U.S. 441 four miles up this little stream. Deep Creek drains 25 percent of the Osceola National Forest and is one of the two areas in the forest where creek swamps are present. It is important to several endangered species because it has extensive mature hardwood stands and very little evidence of human disturbance.

Warning signs begin to appear on trees three-quarters of a mile above the rapids. Big Shoals can be scouted from the left bank and there is a clearly marked trail to follow. At very low water it may be necessary to line the canoe through on the extreme left side. At low- to normal-water levels it can be run against the west bank. The rapids become more aggressive with increased water level and at high water may have standing waves two to three feet high.

The rapid consists of a double drop with the upper drop having a curl coming in from each side so that it has to be run exactly in the middle to keep the boat dry. Thirty yards below the upper drop is another drop of four feet with a standing wave at the bottom. Just below the final drop is a rock, strategically located at the point where paddlers are congratulating themselves on having successfully run the rapids!

Big Shoals is rated a moderate to strenuous rapid depending on the volume of water flowing through it. *It should always be scouted before it is run.* If in doubt about your skill or the turbulence of the water, carry around. In any event it is probably wise to unload your canoe and carry all but your essentials to the bottom of the rapid. *Wear your personal floatation device.* There are large, sharp, limestone boulders in this rapid, and even good swimmers can bump their heads if a canoe capsizes.

Big Shoals is on private property and is not accessible by road without permission. Canoeists camp there, but are dependent on the goodwill of the property owners. Any improper conduct which calls attention to the presence of campers is likely to result in eviction. It is not pleasant to load a canoe and paddle several miles through rocky shoals in the dark. This is also true for picnickers. *Please do your part to keep this area clean and open to your fellow canoeist.*

Robinson Creek enters just below Big Shoals on the east bank. Paddle into it for a very short distance to see an interesting waterfall. Like Deep Creek, it drains from the Osceola National Forest. Bell Springs, the most northern named spring on the Suwannee is located on the east bank. It is on private property, and has been developed for use as a fish pond and swimming pool. Its drainage into the river is not identifiable as a spring run.

Downriver from the shoals, the river returns to its snail pace. Little Shoals, a series of rocky ledges, will be encountered a mile or so upstream from White Springs and serves to liven up the trip. Falling Creek enters from the east at Little Shoals.

U.S. 41 to U.S. 129 at Suwannee Springs (D–E): 17 miles

DIFFICULTY: Easy
SCENERY: Excellent
COUNTY: Suwannee

ACCESS: From White Springs, travel U.S. 41 south to the river. The access is on the northwest side of the bridge—there is a steep, concrete ramp and a wayside park.

TRIP DESCRIPTION: For just one mile the river flows around the town of White Springs to an alternate access on S.R. 136. A canoe livery and campground are in the area between the two bridges. Just below S.R. 136 is the relic of the old springhouse for what used to be called White Sulphur Springs. Records indicate that the first springhouse was built in 1835. The Colonial Hotel and Springhouse, built in the early 1900s, served as a spa and health sanatorium until the 1960s. The spring is enclosed by the concrete foundations of the former bathhouse.

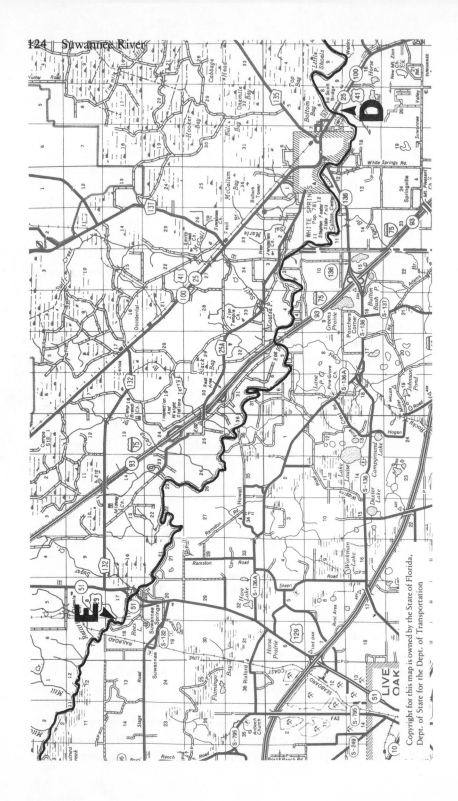

Just north of the spring is the entrance to the Stephen Foster State Folk Culture Center. An annual Folk Festival is held on Memorial Day weekends. There is a museum, carillon tower, picnic tables, restrooms, and shaded walking trails, but no camping facilities.

At White Springs, the river turns and flows to the west. The Florida Trail begins to follow the north bank of the Suwannee from White Springs and will continue to do so to Suwannee River State Park. To the south, S.R. 136A is seldom more than two or three miles away and there are a number of access roads from this side.

Below White Springs the high, limestone banks continue with only an occasional small sandbar. Five miles downriver and within sight of Interstate 75, Swift Creek enters from the north. It is well-named as it rushes through a rocky canyon into the river. It is a charming spot but of questionable safety. Swift Creek carries the waste from a large chemical company a few miles upstream and environmentalists say that it is unwise to swim or fish for several miles below Swift Creek on the Suwannee. The chemical company feels this precaution is not warranted.

Interstate 75 offers no access to the river. It marks the beginning of an area of lower banks and beautiful sandbars.

The high limestone walls are still present, but now the tendency is to have low banks on one side of the river and high banks on the other. At other times, vertical limestone banks on both sides will present graceful corridors that resemble the walls of castles. Caves and grottos have been worn into the rock and the water makes hollow musical sounds as the wake of the canoe moves along the crevices. Occasionally water can be heard dripping far up inside unseen caves inside the walls.

Within three miles of Suwannee Springs there is a small waterfall and a residential community in the woods on the north bank. Fishermen in small boats begin to appear and in the summertime, swimmers and sunbathers frequent the sandbars on the south bank. Despite its popularity, this section is one of the most beautiful and pristine on the entire river.

Suwannee Springs is a town that progress has left behind. There was a post office in the town in 1834; in the early 1880s a resort hotel was built that was said to be one of the finest hostelries in the southeast. A railroad that ran to the front door of the hotel ferried guests back and forth to the town of New Branford where they boarded a paddleboat for the journey to the Gulf. All that is left of this grandeur is the

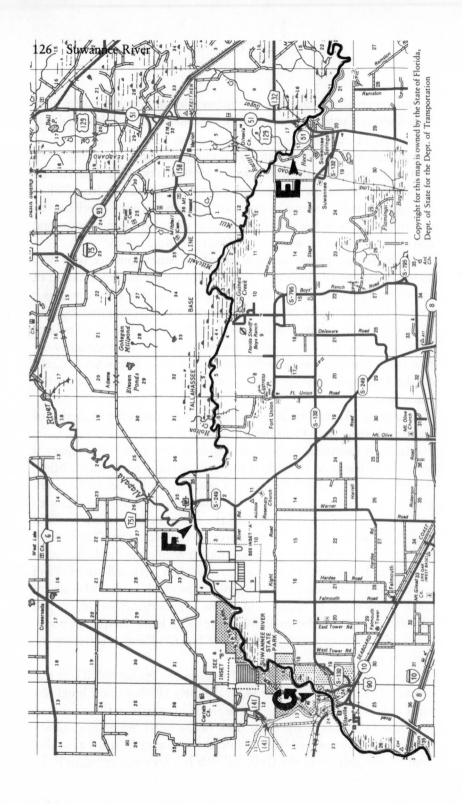

rock retaining wall that separated the springs from the Suwannee River, a few houses, and an abandoned bridge.

At least six springs comprise the Suwannee Springs, four of them outside the wall that confines the main spring. In warm weather this spot is well-populated with swimmers and sunbathers.

Just below Suwannee Springs, the river flows under the unused bridge of old highway 51. There is no access to the river here or at the new bridge a short way below it.

U.S. 129 (below Suwannee Springs) to the Alapaha River (E–F): 13 miles

DIFFICULTY: Easy
SCENERY: Good
COUNTIES: Hamilton, Suwannee

ACCESS: From White Springs, follow S.R. 136 for about three miles until it divides into S.R. 136-A. Follow 136-A for ten miles to the junction with S.R. 51 (U.S. 129). Turn right (north) and continue on U.S. 129 to the Suwannee River, just below the town of Suwannee Springs. Turn left on a dirt road just before reaching the bridge and follow it for one mile to the access.

TRIP DESCRIPTION: There is a railroad trestle just below the put-in and intermittent pastureland for perhaps another mile. A house on the north bank is the only sign of development until one reaches the Florida Sheriffs' Boys Ranch. The high limestone banks continue for several miles but begin to be less noticeable as the river straightens and the banks become sandy and heavily wooded. Sandbars are found only on the inside of sharp bends which are now less common. Campsites are infrequent and would involve carrying gear up high banks into the woods. There is a landing at the ranch which may be used for launching if permission is secured in advance. The Florida Sheriffs' Boys Ranch was founded in 1957 and provides a home for more than one hundred dependent youngsters. A large bell announces mealtimes for the boys and can be heard for a considerable distance on the river.

Holton Creek enters the Suwannee on the north bank about two and one-half miles upstream from the junction with the Alapaha River. Its source is Holton Spring, a first magnitude spring located one mile up the spring run from the Suwannee River. There is also a small spring on the south bank of the river just below the entrance of the creek. Irrigation pipes and other signs of development are evident as well. One-half mile above the confluence of the Alapaha River, another first magnitude spring, Alapaha Rise, enters the river from the north side. This spring appears to consist of a single vent at the head of a depression about 150 feet in diameter. It is at the foot of steep, limestone walls which persist down the 300-foot run to the river. The spring water is a very dark tannin color.

There is some controversy about the location of the actual confluence of the Alapaha River into the Suwannee. A healthy, vigorous river for over one hundred miles through south Georgia, only in times of above normal rainfall does it actually *flow* into the Suwannee. Evidently at some point between Statenville, Georgia, and south of the Florida line, the Alapaha, or some portion of it, goes underground. The result is a clearly-defined riverbed leading into Florida and down to the Suwannee that frequently is either a series of potholes or is completely dry. Local people in this area believe that Alapaha Rise spring is the true resurrection of the Alapaha River.

In any event, the confluence with the riverbed of the Alapaha is one-half mile downstream from the spring. A Hamilton County recreation area, Gibson Park, is located here and a boat ramp, grassy picnic site, and camping area are provided. At one time, a graceful iron bridge spanned the river. In the early 1970s an overloaded truck attempted to cross the bridge and both the bridge and truck settled into the river. In the fall of 1982, surveying was underway to build a new bridge, probably somewhat north of Alapaha Rise.

Alapaha River to Suwannee River State Park (U.S. 90) (F–G): 8 miles

DIFFICULTY: Easy
SCENERY: Good
COUNTY: Suwannee

ACCESS: From Jasper, travel S.R. 6 west and southwest (under Interstate 75) for ten miles to the junction with C.R. 751. Turn south and follow this paved road for less than three miles until it dead-ends into a graded road. Turn east (left) and follow it across the Alapaha River. Less than one mile from the bridge, it will dead-end into another dirt road. Turn south (right) and follow this road to Gibson Park and the

Suwannee River. A newly paved road and bridge across the Suwannee will be forthcoming in the next few years and these directions will alter.

TRIP DESCRIPTION: Below the confluence of the Alapaha, the Suwannee widens even more and houses can be observed on both banks for the next few miles. The boundaries of the state park begin on the west side of the river less than four miles downstream. On the east bank, Lime Spring flows into the river. This run is also called Dry Branch or Dry Run. This is a pleasant spot for one last dip before reaching the Suwannee River State Park.

Just below this spring on the west bank is a privately owned camp store and boat ramp. Hiking trails, campsites, picnicking, water, and electricity are in the state park. Like all Florida state parks, it closes at sundown. If you leave your car parked there, it will be protected, but be sure that you check with the ranger to get the combination to the gate in case you arrive after dark.

Suwannee River State Park (U.S. 90) to the Gulf of Mexico (G–H): 130 miles

DIFFICULTY: Easy
SCENERY: Good
COUNTIES: Suwannee, Madison, Lafayette, Gilchrist, Dixie, Levy

ACCESS: From Live Oak, travel west on U.S. 90 to the Suwannee River State Park sign, turn north and go into the park.

TRIP DESCRIPTION: Below the confluence of the Withlacoochee River and with the advent of a multitude of springs, creeks, and another large river, the Suwannee becomes a truly big river. Paddleboat traffic traversed the river as far north as U.S. 90; now it is frequented by large motorboats. Roads parallel the river on both sides from this point to within 15 miles of the Gulf and access points are plentiful. There are also a number of subdivisions and developments. The river continues to offer some spectacular scenery. A degree of remoteness and the dozens of springs that occur in this section add to its appeal.

Canoeists wishing to paddle this section of the river can easily determine access from a Florida road map. Further information is also available from the Suwannee River Water Management District, P.O. Drawer K, White Springs, FL 32096. Ask for Information Circular 8.

A brief chronology of the primary landmarks on this section follows.

Ellaville Spring is just east of U.S. 90 on the south shore of the river. It flows out of the six-foot-wide mouth of a 30-foot deep cave in a high limestone bluff.

Interstate 10 is about two miles below U.S. 90, no access.

Anderson Spring, just below Interstate 10 on the east bank of the river, is a shallow pool about 50 feet in diameter with a 150-foot run to the Suwannee that is usually dry.

Dowling Park is located where S.R. 250 crosses the Suwannee.

Charles Spring, about six miles south of Dowling Park on the east side of the Suwannee, is an oblong pool divided by a small, limestone natural bridge. Each section has its own boil. Water flows from a pool beneath the limestone about 75 feet to the river.

Allen Mill Pond Spring, seven miles south of Dowling Park on the west side of the river, is a 150-foot-long pond with at least three spring vents. It flows about one-half mile to the river.

Thomas Spring is slightly over a mile south of Charles Spring on the east bank of the Suwannee.

Blue Spring, nine miles south of Dowling Park on the west bank of the Suwannee, consists of two pools, one with the spring boil, the other over a limestone bridge. The clear, dark blue water is from six to ten feet deep.

Perry Spring, less than two miles north of S.R. 51 on the west bank, is a small spring pool with a short run emptying into the Suwannee.

State Road 51 crosses the Suwannee; access is south of the bridge on the east bank.

Telford Spring, one mile east of S.R. 51 on the east bank, is a small, clear pool with a run of 100 feet to the Suwannee. There are houses directly across the river.

Irvine Slough is a swampy area on the east bank of the Suwannee extending from Luraville Springs, due north of Telford Spring, for about a mile downriver to the vicinity of Peacock Slough.

Peacock Slough empties into the Suwannee from the east bank one and one-half miles downstream from S.R. 51. Bonnet Spring and Peacock Spring are its source, one and one-half miles north. Also in the vicinity, but not feeding directly into Peacock Slough are Pump Spring, Baptizing Spring, Walker Spring, and Orange Grove Spring.

Cow Spring is three miles downstream from S.R. 51 on the north bank of a large bend in the river. It is an oval pool with angular boulders visible through the clear water.

Running Springs are less than a mile downstream from Cow Spring on the same side of the river. Two springs on either side of a dirt road, they have steep limestone walls, numerous boils, and limestone bridges.

Convict Spring is four miles from S.R. 51 on the southwest bank of the Suwannee. The spring vent is in the northern end of a 20- by 50-foot teardrop-shaped pool that has been enclosed with a concrete wall.

Royal Spring is four and one-half miles from S.R. 51 on the north side of the Suwannee. The pool is 200 feet long by 100 feet wide with a concrete retaining wall on the east side.

Suwannee Blue Spring, a fenced spring, is less than a half mile from Royal Spring on the same side of the river.

Owens Spring, eleven miles downriver from S.R. 51 on the west bank of the Suwannee, is an oval pool with limestone outcrops and dark blue green water. The run flows 150 feet into the river but disappears and emerges through potholes. It eventually enters the river through a vent in the riverbed a few yards out from the mouth of the run. There is an access to the river at Owens Spring from S.R. 251.

Mearson (or Morrison) Spring is just south of Owens Spring. A 25-by-50-foot pool surrounded by high banks, it discharges about 75 feet into the Suwannee.

Troy Spring is about five miles above Branford on the southwest side of the Suwannee. An elongated pool 50 to 75 feet wide with almost vertical side walls, this spring is 80 feet deep in places. The water is usually clear and the submerged hull of the steamboat *Madison* can be seen, its bow pointing toward the head of the spring. Local sources claim that the *Madison* was a supply ship of the Confederate Army that was trapped on the river and run aground by its captain to prevent capture. It is a first magnitude spring pumping 66 million gallons of water daily.

Little River Springs is three miles above U.S. 27 at Branford on the north side of the river. The water is clear and blue. The vent is the entrance to a cave system more than 1,200 feet long and 100 feet deep.

Ruth Spring, south of Troy Spring on the same side of the river, has a pool 50 feet in diameter that is clear with a sandy bottom.

U.S. 27 at Branford—the access is to the south of the bridge at Branford.

Branford Springs is southeast of the junction of U.S. 27 and U.S. 129 at the town of Branford. It is part of a recreational area with swimming, picnicking, restrooms, and a boat ramp. Its run flows 75 feet to the Suwannee River. Branford Springs is said to pump 6.8 million gallons daily.

Junction with the Santa Fe River—ten miles south of Branford, the Santa Fe enters from the east side. If the Suwannee is the *Queen of Rivers*, the Santa Fe is the *Princess*. There are seventeen named springs on the Santa Fe and nine named springs on its tributary the Ichetucknee River. Both have dozens of unnamed springs. The confluence of the Santa Fe opens up the river to even bigger boats, races, and waterskiing.

Fletcher Spring and Turtle Spring are a little over two miles south of the confluence with the Santa Fe, on the west bank of the Suwannee. Fletcher Spring has an oval pool and a clear, greenish tint. Turtle Spring is keyhole-shaped, surrounded by swampy woods, and reported to be 25 feet deep with tunnels branching back 60 to 70 feet.

Rock Bluff Spring is about three miles north of S.R. 340, on the east side of the Suwannee River. It is a large pool near the site of an old ferry crossing. Now privately owned, it pumps 27 million gallons daily.

State Road 340 Bridge—access is from a wayside park north of the bridge on the east bank.

Guaranto Spring, less than two miles below S.R. 340 on the west bank, is an oblong pool 240 by 80 feet. It is now the site of a county park with swimming, camping, and other facilities.

Sun Springs (or Aiken Springs), 11 miles south of S.R. 340 on the east bank of the river, is a long pool with clear blue green water. The run from Lumbercamp Springs joins its run.

Hart Springs is two springs nine miles above U.S. 19 on the east bank. Both have been enclosed in concrete pools as a part of the Gilchrist County Recreational Area; swimming and camping is permitted.

Otter Springs is about two miles downstream from Hart Springs on the east bank of the Suwannee. It is also two pools separated by a run. There is a private campground with swimming, fishing, and boating permitted.

McCrabb Spring is a small spring on the west bank of the Suwannee.

Little Copper Spring, four miles above U.S. 19 on the west bank, is a small pool with a narrow run. The water is clear but has a strong sulphur odor. A reddish brown iron deposit gives it its name.

Copper Spring (Old Town Spring) is nearly one mile downriver from Little Copper. It is three privately owned springs that have been improved with culverts and a concrete dock.

Bell Springs, less than one mile above U.S. 19 at the town of Fanning Springs, is at the northwest end of an unnamed tributary to the Suwannee.

U.S. 19 crosses the Suwannee River at the town of Fanning Springs. It is the last bridge to cross the Suwannee River before reaching the Gulf. Access is from a wayside park on the south side of the bridge on the east bank. There is a private campground and launching facility on the west bank.

Big Fanning Spring and Little Fanning Spring are just south of U.S. 19 at the town of Fanning Springs on the east bank of the Suwannee. These are large spring pools that were highly developed at one time with a dancing and skating pavilion, bathhouses, and a diving tower. It is now privately owned and not generally open to the public.

Manatee Springs, seven miles south of U.S. 19, is the site of one of the most beautiful parks in Florida. On the east side of the river, it discharges 109 million gallons of water daily through a 1,200-foot run. An extensive cave system is said to extend eastward from the spring boil. Camping, boating, swimming, and recreational facilities are available.

Fowler Bluff, ten miles below U.S. 19, on the east bank, is the last good access to the Suwannee River before reaching the Gulf. For the next seventeen miles, the banks are swampy and remote and the river becomes very tidal and scattered among hammocks, islands, and passes.

Suwannee is located on the west bank at the mouth of the Gulf of Mexico.

TAKE-OUT: There are many access points on this 130-mile stretch. For those paddling to the Gulf, the last access is at the town of Suwannee. From U.S. 27-A/98/19, just west of the Suwannee River at Fanning Springs, turn south on S.R. 349 and continue 25 miles to Suwannee.
COUNTY MAPS: Hamilton, Columbia, Suwannee, Madison, Lafayette, Gilchrist, Dixie, Levy

Santa Fe River

The Santa Fe is one of the most beautiful and unusual waterways in north Florida as well as being of considerable historical interest. It serves as the county line for Alachua County, dividing it from the neighboring counties of Bradford, Union, and Columbia. It begins in the Santa Fe lakes in the extreme northeast corner of Alachua County, flows through Santa Fe swamp, and then veers in a northwesterly direction toward O'Leno State Park where it goes underground. For its first eighteen miles it is a tiny meandering stream that is not navigable. At Worthington Springs it becomes minimally canoeable for the very determined, and at S.R. 241, just a few miles above O'Leno State Park, it becomes a pleasant stream for even the novice paddler. At O'Leno, the river goes underground in a lazy whirlpool and follows subterranean passageways for some three miles to River Rise State Preserve. When the Santa Fe returns, it is as a generously-sized river some 75 to 100 feet wide. This area, from O'Leno to River Rise is owned primarily by the state of Florida, either as O'Leno State Park or as the River Rise State Preserve and is laced with excellent hiking trails. The natural bridge provided by the Santa Fe at this point was one of the primary crossing points offered to Indians and early settlers. As a result, several very old roadbeds including Bellamy road and Wire road cross this area. Many interesting artifacts have been discovered by hikers on these trails.

From the river to the confluence of the Suwannee, the Santa Fe is said to have over three dozen springs, many of them of the first magnitude. The Ichetucknee River, a tributary of the Santa Fe, is a paradise of crystal clear springs. Because of its popularity with tubers, it is better known and more highly populated. The terrain surrounding the Santa Fe possesses almost every plant community known to the northcentral Florida area. It has sandhills, swamps, flatwoods, and hardwood hammocks. The protection of the state-owned land has made a refuge for deer, turkey, otter, bobcat, and other animals indigenous to north Florida.

Worthington Springs to State Road 241 (A–B): 6 miles

DIFFICULTY: Strenuous
SCENERY: Good
COUNTIES: Union, Alachua

134

ACCESS: From the town of Worthington Springs, travel south on S.R. 121 to the bridge. Access is on the northwest side of the bridge off a sandy, deeply rutted road.

TRIP DESCRIPTION: At one time Worthington Springs was the site of a hotel, swimming pool, bathhouse, and recreation hall. Nothing remains now except the ruins of the concrete pool that contains the spring. The pool is located in a low wooded area on the north bank of the river just below the put-in.

Although the river is 50 to 75 feet wide at this point, clear of obstructions, and flowing at a leisurely pace, its canoeable appearance is deceiving. Shortly below S.R. 241, the river begins to be obstructed with willow trees that offer a challenge in maneuvering as the lazy current picks up speed. After practicing in the small willow tangles, the paddler will be prepared for the more technical, Confusion Willow Swamp. The channel splits again and again as it enters a mile long tangle of willow trees. This section of the Santa Fe should only be paddled in normal to high water in the winter when the branches are bare by those determined canoeists who want to paddle a river from its highest put-in point.

State Road 241 to O'Leno State Park (B–C): 5 miles

DIFFICULTY: Moderate
SCENERY: Good
COUNTIES: Union, Columbia, Alachua

ACCESS: From the town of Alachua proceed north on S.R. 241 for ten miles to the bridge across the Santa Fe. Access is on the northwest side of the bridge off a poorly maintained road.

TRIP DESCRIPTION: After emerging from the willow swamp above S.R. 241, the river becomes deep and slow and is a dark tannin collor, like strongly brewed tea. The banks are steep with occasional. swampy areas and rare, small sandbars on the curves. There are a few houses scattered on this section and some pastureland on the higher banks.

With the advent of Olustee Creek, the river widens to 100 feet and is deep with ten to fifteen foot high banks. There is a road and boat ramp at this point but it is on private property and is not a public access. Olustee Creek is said to be canoeable at very high-water levels.

It is slightly over a mile from the confluence of Olustee Creek to

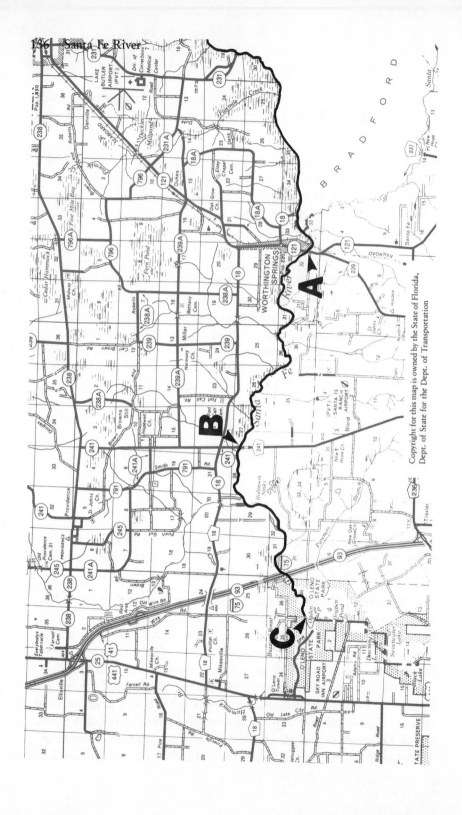

Interstate 75. There is no access but shortly below the interstate bridge there is a concrete boat ramp on the northwest side. This access is reached from U.S. 41/441.

Below the interstate the river narrows again and enters O'Leno State Park. It is now about 75 feet wide with banks four to six feet high. There is a rocky shoal that provides a little interest just above the take-out at the park. There are three shoals on the river below the take-out but the canoeist has to paddle back up river after running them, since the river goes underground shortly below the take-out downstream from O'Leno.

TAKE-OUT (C): From the town of Lake City, travel south on U.S. 41/441 for 16 miles to the entrance to O'Leno State Park. The park closes at sundown, so make arrangements with the ranger if you feel you may be late getting off the river.

U.S. 41/441 (State Road 25) to River Rise (D–D): 4 miles round trip

DIFFICULTY: Easy
SCENERY: Good
COUNTY: Columbia

ACCESS: From the town of High Springs, travel northwest on U.S. 41/441 for about two miles to the bridge across the Santa Fe. Access is on the northwest side of the bridge. There is a boat ramp on the southeast side of the river. It is reached by turning left (west) onto a paved road just before reaching the bridge. There is also a canoe livery right at the river on the southeast side of the bridge. Canoe rental, shuttle service, and launching are available for a fee.

TRIP DESCRIPTION: It is only two miles upstream from the U.S. 41/441 access to River Rise and since almost all of the property on both sides of the river is owned by the state, it is a remote and beautiful trip. The current is bracing paddling upstream, but canoeists can lessen the work by ferrying back and forth with the current to remain on the inside bends and by watching behind downed trees for eddys in which to rest. Very efficient paddlers make the trip in less than 45 minutes, less experienced canoeists may choose to rest more and take an hour or two. In any event, coming back downstream is a breeze and the scenery is worth the effort.

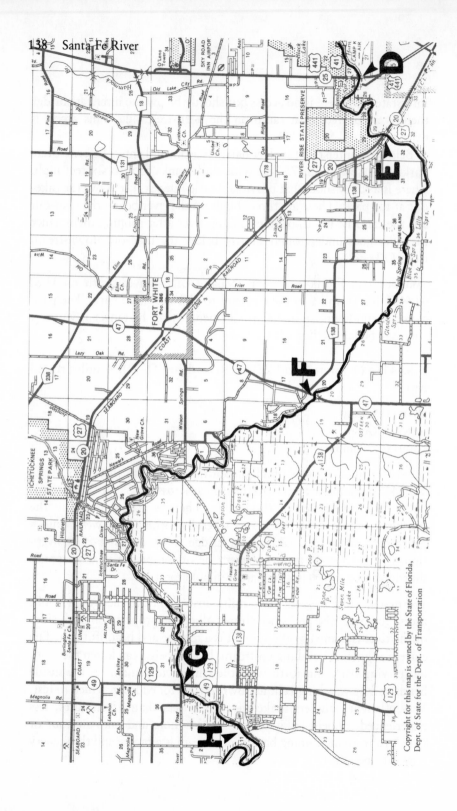

At River Rise, the river suddenly reappears from underground, about 100 feet wide and flowing swiftly. Several trails meet at this point and there is a pleasant grassy glade for picnicking or camping. The banks around the rise are four to six feet high and heavily wooded. Paddling downstream, the banks rise ten to twelve feet in places and are very swampy in others. Just above and within sight of the U.S. 41/441 bridge, a spring run on the left (south) bank indicates the entrance to Darby and Hornsby Springs. Darby Spring is just inside this run and the banks around it are private property.

Hornsby Spring is almost one mile further northwest up this run. The main spring is a part of Camp Kulaqua, a privately owned facility, that is highly developed with diving platforms, sliding boards, and retaining walls. It is probably best not to paddle into the springhead itself. The run is very beautiful, however, and there are several smaller spring boils along the way. Paddlers who chose to canoe up this run should be aware that Camp Kulaqua has a small private zoo and the roar of lions and tigers can be unnerving to the uninitiated.

U.S. 41/441 (State Road 25) to U.S. 27 (D–E): 3 miles

DIFFICULTY: Easy
SCENERY: Good
COUNTIES: Columbia, Gilchrist, Alachua

ACCESS: From the town of High Springs travel northwest on U.S. 41/441 for about two miles to the bridge across the Santa Fe. Access is on the northwest side of the bridge. There is a boat ramp on the southeast side of the river, reached by turning left (west) onto a paved road just before reaching the bridge. There is also a canoe livery right at the river on the southeast side of the bridge.

TRIP DESCRIPTION: The Santa Fe is wide at this access, 100 to 150 feet with banks varying from 5 to 12 feet high. The current is slow and the water is generally clear at low-water levels, 5 to 15 feet deep, and without sandbars. There are several shallow shoals and at low water there is a spot where the river divides and half of it disappears into a sink near the north bank. It reappears in a boil in mid-river a few hundred yards downstream.

U.S. 27 to State Road 47 (E–F): 10 miles

DIFFICULTY: Easy
SCENERY: Excellent
COUNTY: Columbia

ACCESS: From High Springs travel three miles north on U.S. 27 to the river. The access is on the north side of the bridge.

TRIP DESCRIPTION: This section of the river is very popular with canoeists and divers because of the vast array of beautiful springs. The river is occasionally shallow and the occurrence of rocky shoals makes it undesirable for large motorboats. In addition, low swampy terrain makes it unsuitable for housing developments and, for the time being, it is one of the loveliest spots in Florida.

There are a few houses scattered along the higher banks just below U.S. 27, but they are soon passed by. Allen Spring is located on the right bank about one and one-half miles downstream from U.S. 27, and at low-water level, a number of small, unnamed springs may also be seen. Across the river, on the left bank, a quarter of a mile downstream, is Poe Spring. A large spring boil flowing from a horizontal cavern with several smaller boils nearby, this spring forms a circular pool about 90 feet in diameter. It is connected to the river by a 175-foot run. At one time there was commercial development here but no evidence of it remains. It is still a popular swimming and picnicking spot, however. Poe Spring marks the beginning of lowland and swampy areas along the banks that are spotted with small springs.

Lilly Spring is located less than a mile from Poe Spring on the left bank. Jonathan Spring will be on the right bank just before reaching an island in the river. At the end of the island, watch the right bank for Rum Island Spring. The Blue Spring run will be seen entering the river from the left bank. Paddle 500 feet up the run to the spring. This is a privately owned area and canoes are not permitted to paddle over the spring vent. Nearby, in the swamp around Blue Spring are Little Blue Spring, Johnson Spring, and Naked Spring.

Less than three miles downriver are July Spring on the right bank and Devil's Eye and Devil's Ear springs on the left. These springs discharge from a system of caverns and passages said to be more than 1,000 feet long and up to 95 feet deep. Devil's Eye and Devil's Ear are connected with July Spring across the river.

Just a quarter of a mile further is Ginnie Spring, a large oval pool that is 50 feet deep and is said to be undermined by an extensive cave system with some 1,000 feet of passages.

The area from July and the Devil springs to below Ginnie Spring is owned by the Ginnie Spring Corporation. There is an extensive private campground, boardwalks, and facilities for scuba divers.

A mile below Ginnie Spring one encounters the first of four rocky shoals across the river. The springs have contributed a considerable current to the river but none of the shoals are difficult to maneuver. An island just below the first shoal should be run on the southwest side.

The water on this section is clear at normal- to low-water levels with water weeds on the bottom and reddish-colored pebbles in the depressions in the rocks. Cypress and other lowland hardwoods are prevalent in the swampy areas. Campsites are limited both because of the posted property and the swampy terrain. In addition to the commerical campground at Ginnie Spring, it is also possible to camp at places where roads come down to the river or on unposted land on the north bank.

State Road 47 to U.S. 129 (F–G): 13 miles

DIFFICULTY: Easy
SCENERY: Good
COUNTIES: Gilchrist, Suwannee

ACCESS: From Fort White travel south on S.R. 47 for about six miles until reaching the Santa Fe River. The access is on the southeast side of the bridge.

TRIP DESCRIPTION: From S.R. 47 to U.S. 129, there are roads and sub-divisions very near the river on the right bank and one is seldom out of sight of a house. The banks begin to be higher, and there are three rocky shoals above the confluence of the Ichetucknee. These shoals limit large motorboat traffic for the first three miles, but after the Ichetucknee enters the Santa Fe, the river is likely to be crowded with a great deal of motor traffic including ski boats. There are several boat ramps along this section on the right bank.

Northbank Spring is located about one-half mile downstream from S.R. 47 on the right bank. Wilson Spring is one and one-half miles farther down and the boat ramp at Wilson Spring road is the last public access before the confluence of the Ichetucknee. After the Ichetucknee comes in, the Santa Fe widens even more and the river is deeper and less clear. Despite the presence of roads and houses, this is not a heavily populated area and there are a number of pocket swamps along the way that are teeming with bird life. One winter day, a group of canoeists saw an American bald eagle on this section.

U.S. 129/S.R. 49 to the Suwannee River (G–H): 2 miles

DIFFICULTY: Easy
SCENERY: Good
COUNTIES: Suwannee, Gilchrist

ACCESS: From Branford, travel east on U.S. 27 four miles to the intersection with U.S. 129/S.R. 49. Turn right (south) on S.R. 49 and continue two and one-half miles to the bridge over the Santa Fe. Access is on the northeast side of the bridge. Another access is at Sandy Point, one-quarter mile downriver from the S.R. 49 bridge on the north bank.

TRIP DESCRIPTION: This trip is for those who want to say that they did the whole thing. This is a wide, windy stretch of river that is crowded with every kind of motorized watercraft. There are some interesting springs, however, including the Pleasant Grove Springs on the left bank just above the confluence with the Suwannee.

TAKE-OUT (H): There is no access at the confluence of the Suwannee and the Santa Fe, but there is a boat landing on the southside of the Santa Fe less than a half mile from the confluence. To reach it, cross the Santa Fe on the S.R. 49 bridge and drive south for one mile to the first graded road that turns right. Turn right and continue to the river.

Ichetucknee River

The Ichetucknee River raises the question of how does one discriminate a river from a creek, or even a spring run. From its beginning at Ichetucknee Spring, to its confluence with the Santa Fe River, it is less than six miles, yet it is officially designated as a *river*. By any name, Ichetucknee is one of the most scenic waterways in north Florida. There are nine named and many unnamed springs along the first three and one-half miles of this river. They provide a leisurely current that makes paddling effortless over the crystal clear water, white sand bottom, and the myriad spring vents and pools.

Ichetucknee Springs State Park to U.S. 27 (A–B): 3.5 miles

DIFFICULTY: Easy
SCENERY: Superb
COUNTIES: Suwannee, Columbia

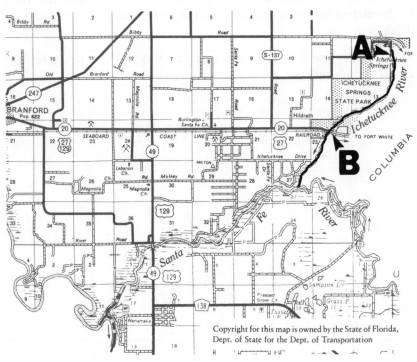

Copyright for this map is owned by the State of Florida, Dept. of State for the Dept. of Transportation

ACCESS: From Branford, travel east on U.S. 129/27 to the signs directing you to Ichetucknee Springs State Park. Follow the signs to the park and the Ichetucknee Spring.

TRIP DESCRIPTION: The canoe trail begins at Ichetucknee Springs State Park and is not accessible during the summer months. The springs begin with the Ichetucknee or Head Spring, and in downstream order are Cedar Head, Blue Hole, Roaring, Singing, Boiling, Grassy Hole, Mill Pond and Coffee springs. Alligator Creek and Rose Creek flow near the Ichetucknee and disappear into sinkholes north of the springs. As you paddle, you will find other springs that are unnamed.

Ichetucknee is a tuber's paradise and access to the river is controlled by park rangers. The trail and park ends three and one-half miles south at U.S. 27. The paddler who completes the remaining two miles then must paddle down the Santa Fe some four miles to the next access. This can be a long and windy trip. Since no food or beverages are permitted in canoes traversing the river through the park, arrangements should be made to take on provisions when the canoes reach U.S. 27. From October through March or April, canoeists usually have the river to themselves but must still observe the regulations against food and drink.

TAKE-OUT (B): Travel from Branford east on U.S. 129/27 to the bridge across the Ichetucknee.

The Central Peninsula

Withlacoochee (South)

Photograph by John Pearce

The Withlacoochee (South)

The Withlacoochee River, south, is said to have been named after its sister river to the north, but the two rivers are separated by many miles and bear little resemblance to each other. The southern Withlacoochee, one of Florida's finest touring rivers, is over 100 miles long with 84 miles of good canoeing trail. While there is a great deal of development along some of its banks, there are also long stretches of beautiful and remote wilderness. In addition, the characteristics of the river are continually changing so that every day of paddling presents a new and different river experience.

The Withlacoochee can be found on maps in the extreme southern section of Sumter County as a tiny stream wandering through the Withlacoochee Swamp. It becomes a clearly defined waterway after leaving Green Swamp in the Richloam Wildlife Management Area of the Withlacoochee State Forest, and flows north to the Gulf of Mexico at Yankeetown.

The diversity of the vegetation and wildlife is a reflection of the constantly changing terrain of the river. Beginning in cypress and hardwood swamp, it progresses through upland hardwood and pine forests, past cypress ponds, palmetto hammocks and landscaped backyards. The Tsala Apopka Lake region is a miniature Everglades with an abundance of birds and reptiles, hammocks of water weeds, and multi-faceted channels. Fishing is excellent along the river but game animals are now scarce except in isolated pockets. Certain sections of the river are easily accessible and are heavily populated during the warm months of the year. Other sections appear to have been abandoned to an occasional air boat and the canoeist.

Coulter Hammock Recreation Area to State Road 50 (A–B): 12 miles

DIFFICULTY: Easy
SCENERY: Good
COUNTIES: Pasco, Hernando

ACCESS: From Lacoochee, travel east on S.R. 575. Turn south on Lacoochee Park road and continue for about two miles to the entrance to the state forest. Continue for less than one mile to the river.

TRIP DESCRIPTION: For the first two miles, the river flows through a remote and undeveloped part of the state forest. At S.R. 575 there is a

147

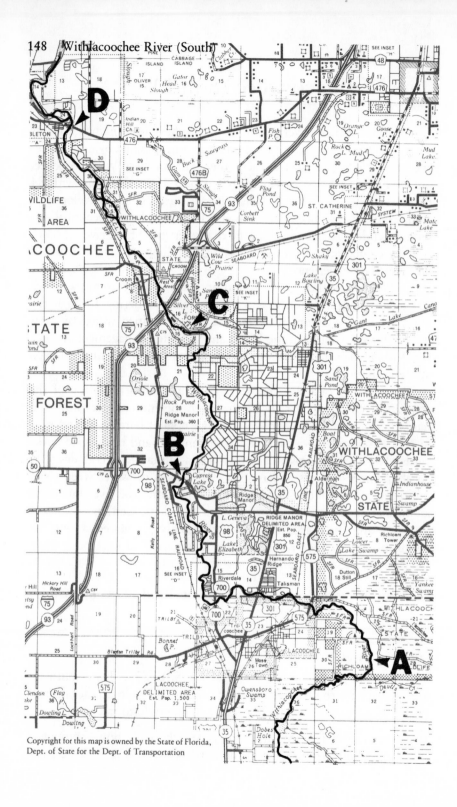

rough access on the right bank above the bridge and just below the bridge on the left bank is a conoe livery.

The river is usually shallow in this area, about 35 feet wide with a slow to moderate current. The banks vary from 6 to 15 feet high and there are a number of small, rocky shoals across the river. There are houses scattered along this section and campsites are scarce. The canoe camper should watch carefully for the few small sandbars that will accommodate one or two tents.

There is a railroad trestle shortly below S.R. 575 and there are accesses at U.S. 301 and at U.S. 98. From U.S. 98 north to S.R. 50, U.S. 98 is seldom more than one mile from the river on the right side.

State Road 50 to Silver Lake (B–C): 7 miles

DIFFICULTY: Easy
SCENERY: Good
COUNTY: Hernando

ACCESS: From Brooksville, travel 12 miles east on S.R. 50 to the river. The access is on the southwest side of the bridge.

TRIP DESCRIPTION: There are a number of houses during the first mile below S.R. 50, but they decrease in frequency as the river enters the Croom Wildlife Management Area of the state forest. The banks began to be lower and the frequency of sandbars increases. The banks are primarily covered with highland hardwoods and pine forest, but some small swampy areas begin to occur as well. The river continues to be shallow with little current. There are three large state forest campgrounds in the vicinity of Silver Lake with electricity, running water, and showers. The Little Withlacoochee enters from the east just before reaching Silver Lake and as a result, the river widens to 50 to 75 feet.

Silver Lake to State Road 476 (C–D): 9 miles

DIFFICULTY: Easy
SCENERY: Good
COUNTIES: Hernando, Sumter

ACCESS: From Brooksville, travel east on S.R. 50 for about eight miles. Pass under Interstate 75 then one mile further to the first paved road to the left, a state forest road. Continue on this road for about three

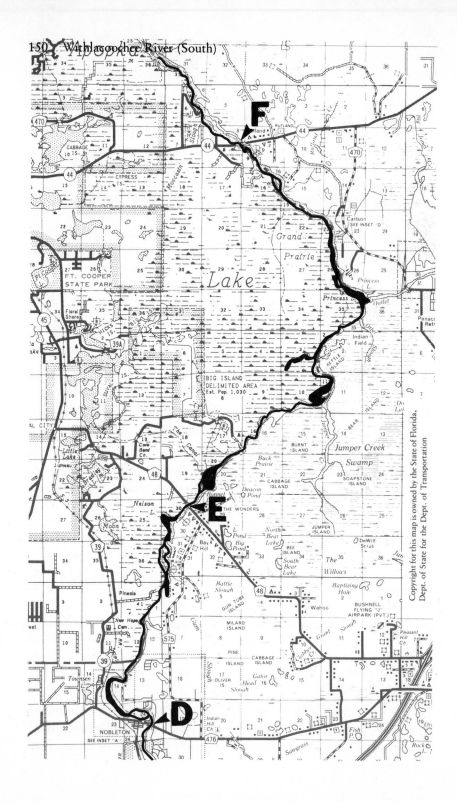

miles to just before reaching the interstate again. Turn right on a graded road that parallels the interstate that leads to a boat ramp on the river at Silver Lake.

TRIP DESCRIPTION: Silver Lake is three-quarters of a mile long and one-half mile wide. Interstate 75 is visible as soon as one enters the lake and since the river flows under the interstate, one should paddle toward it. The water is very shallow at the dual bridges but deepens as the river narrows to about 40 feet wide on the other side. The banks are three to four feet high with numerous campsites under the trees. The color of the river darkens in this area and it is said to be a good section for fishing. After reaching Hog Island, the banks become lower. The river splits around Hog Island, but is navigable either way. Houses become evident again just south of S.R. 476, the water becomes shallow and choked with water weeds, and the river widens to 150 feet.

State Road 476 to State Road 48 (D–E): 9 miles

DIFFICULTY: Easy
SCENERY: Good
COUNTY: Sumter

ACCESS: From Brooksville, travel north on S.R. 45 (U.S. 41) for about five miles to the intersection of S.R. 476. Turn right and continue for four miles to the river. The access is on the southeast side of the bridge.

TRIP DESCRIPTION: One-half mile below this access the river divides with the left channel leading to Nobelton Park. The crossing of the old Fort King road is on the south side of the river, just east of Nobelton Park. The fort, built in 1837, was named for Major Francis Langhorne Dade. It was an observation post and supply depot for troops stationed in the area. On 6 March 1837, the Seminole Indian leaders, Jumper and Alligator, met with General Thomas Jessup to sign a treaty that ended one of the longest and bloodiest Indian wars in Amerian history.

North of Nobelton the river undergoes a drastic change as it enters a series of large lakes. These lakes are shallow and clogged with water weeds, but have abundant bird life and numerous alligators. On the higher ground, a few houses are scattered but it is a reasonably remote section.

State Road 48 to State Road 44 (E–F): 15 miles

DIFFICULTY: Easy
SCENERY: Excellent
COUNTIES: Sumter, Citrus, Hernando

ACCESS: From Brooksville, travel north on S.R. 45 for about eight miles to the intersection with S.R. 48. Turn right and continue to the river. The access is on the southeast side of the bridge.

TRIP DESCRIPTION: This section of the Withlacoochee flows through the Tsala Apopka Lake region, a series of lakes and swamps that continues for some 18 miles. There is seldom any current to follow; the river often wanders off among small channels, islands, and hammocks. It is one of the most beautiful and the most remote part of this river. The number and variety of bird life is astonishing and the cypress-ringed lakes and swampy hammocks provide a true wilderness experience. Campsites are scarce and road access to the river is very limited.

Just north of S.R. 48, the river enters Bonnet Lake which is over a mile long. There is a private landing on the southwest side of the lake and at the northwest end a boat rental and camp appropriately named Trail's End. The river deepens and is 50 to 75 feet wide when it leaves the lake. A mile north of Bonnet Lake is Board Island. Reputed to be the last highground available for many miles, it is covered with palmettos and would be a dubious campsite at best. Just one-half mile north of Board Island is a good campsite on Shell Island.

After leaving Board Island, the river turns east and opens into a small lake with an arm reaching to the south. About one-third of the way down this arm on the east bank is a shack on pilings and a concrete boat ramp. There are about four acres of highground here with huge oaks and some old orange trees. This property is owned by the State of Florida but has no public access by road. Shell Island is not an island surrounded by water, but by a large swamp known as The Wanderings. Persons with permission to cross private property use this area for camping and fishing.

After leaving this small lake, the river widens to 150 to 200 feet with a meandering channel about 30 feet wide that is not choked by weeds. Another mile of paddling reveals a larger lake with an arm to the south where Jumper Creek enters the river. This creek is canoeable but originates in swamp and has no access. Past Jumper Creek, the stream turns north and one should stay on the east side of the three small islands in the river. Soon, a pasture appears on the west side that continues for over one mile and there are occasional canals and rough tracks that indicate that houses may be nearby although they are not visible from the river. Soon another large, shallow lake begins and the overflow from Lake Panasoffkee comes in from the east. The channel is less clear as the river is overgrown with water weeds. Going west, the lake narrows and some houses are visible, set well back from the water line. This wide, shallow area continues to the Ruff Wysong Dam and Navigation Lock. Operated by the Southwest Florida Water Management District, this dam has a unique "water bag" lock construction. The "bag" is made of fabric and the lock is raised and lowered by pumping water into and out of the bag. The dam itself is about 300 feet long and deceptively shallow. The lock tender at the dam reported that some canoeists do paddle over the dam but few are successful in staying upright. Man-made obstructions such as dams present a smooth hydraulic that can be very dangerous.

There are a number of houses and a small community at the site of the dam. The shallow lake continues for another two and one-half miles. This is one of the shallowest sections of the entire river and during very dry weather it may be necessary to walk the canoe in some areas.

State Road 44 to State Road 200 (F–G): 16 miles

DIFFICULTY: Easy
SCENERY: Good
COUNTIES: Citrus, Sumter

ACCESS: From Inverness, travel six and one-half miles due east on S.R. 44. The access is on the southeast side of the bridge.

TRIP DESCRIPTION: North of S.R. 44, the river becomes deeper and is 150 to 200 feet wide and lined with hardwood swamps. The river will occasionally narrow to 100 feet and there will be short stretches of high ground, but there is little current. Scattered homesites as well as small communities of riverside homes are evident all along this section, and campsites are few. There is a public access at the boat ramp off S.R. 581 with boat rentals and a store. Immediately north of S.R. 581, on the east bank is the entrance to the Gum Slough. This slough flows into the Withlacoochee from Gum Springs, about five miles to

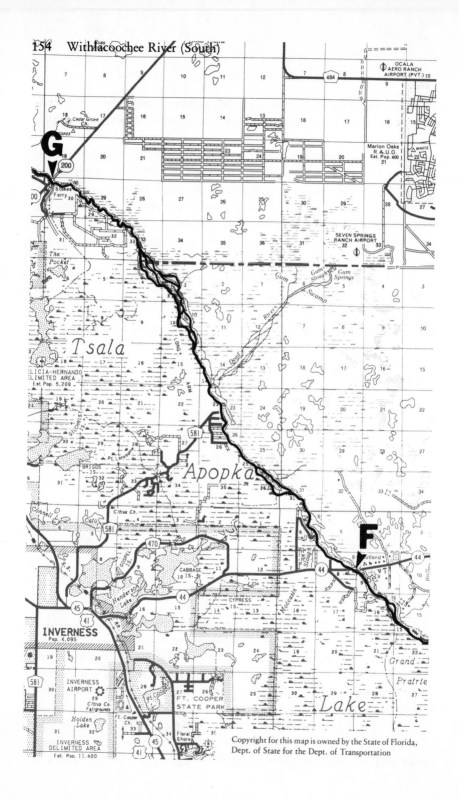

the northwest. Gum Springs are a group of at least seven individual springs located on private property and are not accessible to the public. Gum Slough has been fenced shortly above the point of its confluence with the river. This fence is currently the subject of litigation (1984).

The confluence of Gum Slough adds a little current to the river and it continues at about 100 feet wide for another mile. It then begins to divide around hardwood islands that are low and swampy. The canoeist can stay on the west side of these islands and enjoy a beautiful and remote hardwood swamp filled with wading birds, osprey and alligators, as well as very tall pond cypress trees.

As the swampy area decreases, houses begin to appear on the west side of the river and are scattered along at irregular intervals until S.R. 200 is sighted. There are very few campsites in this entire 16-mile section since the terrain that is not swampy tends to be posted private property. It is possible to find an occasional spot for one or two tents, but one should watch carefully, take advantage of a site when one is spotted, and not plan to camp a large group.

State Road 200 to U.S. 41 at Dunnellon (G–H): 15 miles

DIFFICULTY: Easy
SCENERY: Good
COUNTIES: Citrus, Marion

ACCESS: From Hernando, travel six and one-half miles north on S.R. 200 to the river. The access is from a wayside park and boat ramp on the northeast side of the bridge.

TRIP DESCRIPTION: The modest current continues north of S.R. 200 and the banks are from 4 to 10 feet high, with houses scattered along the way. There are numerous campsites along this section, but they are obviously accessible by road and tend to be littered. The river is 75 to 100 feet wide and twists through gentle curves and high banks for about five miles before opening into a large swamp again. This wide swampy area, with water weeds and fingers of water reaching into cypress stands, is very beautiful and should be relished as one enters the final miles of the canoe trail.

At the northeast end of the swamp, small hills appear and the houses begin again. The Blue Run from Rainbow Springs enters from the north just one mile before reaching Dunnellon and the take-out.

Copyright for this map is owned by the State of Florida,
Dept. of State for the Dept. of Transportation

TAKE-OUT (H): The take-out is located at the public wayside park in the town of Dunnellon. Below Dunnellon the Withlacoochee becomes Lake Rousseau, a man-made impoundment created by the dam at Inglis Lake. After leaving Lake Rousseau, it winds its way to the Gulf of Mexico at Yankeetown. The lower section of the river is highly developed and heavily used by large motorboats.

Streams in the Ocala National Forest

The Ocala National Forest, established in 1908, covers 378,000 acres of the Central Highlands of north central Florida. Forestation includes the largest area of sand pines in the world as well as hardwood hammocks and swampy palm and palmetto bogs. There are over six hundred lakes and ponds in the forest and myriad crystal clear springs. The Oklawaha River flows through parts of the federally owned land and the Juniper and Alexander springs runs are surrounded by the forest. This is a very popular recreation area and canoeists do not have the privacy on these streams that they have further north. The waterways are of unique and unusual beauty, however, and it is well worthwhile to share the wealth with others.

Information about canoeing and camping in the Ocala National Forest may be obtained from the U.S. Department of Agriculture, Forest Service, Southern Region, P.O. Box 1050, Tallahassee, FL 32302.

Alexander Springs and Alexander Springs Creek

Alexander Springs Recreation Area to boat ramp on Alexander Creek (A–B): 7 miles

DIFFICULTY: Easy
SCENERY: Superb
COUNTY: Lake

ACCESS: From the town of Astor, travel west on S.R. 40 to the intersection with S.R. 445. Turn left (south) and continue for about four miles to the entrance to Alexander Springs Recreation Area.

TRIP DESCRIPTION: Alexander Springs is a first magnitude spring with a flow of 76 million gallons daily. The springhead is in a large pool about two hundred feet in diameter that is a popular swimming area. For the first five miles, the stream is wide and slow moving and it is possible to turn back at any point and paddle against the current to the springhead.

Below Ellis Landing, the stream becomes narrower and more winding and is frequently divided by hammocks of palms and other vegetation.

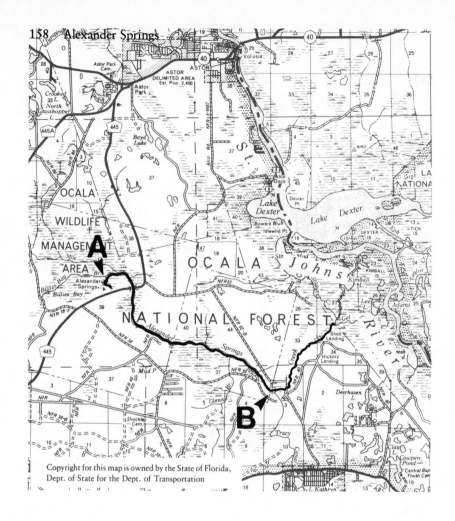

There may also be jams of water hyacinths. It becomes a broad, slow moving stream again before entering the St. Johns River. It is best for the canoeist not to paddle on to the St. Johns since it is several miles up the river to a landing. Canoes can be rented from the concessionaire at Alexander Springs Recreation Area, but no shuttle service is available.

TAKE-OUT (B): From Alexander Springs travel north on C.R. 445 for ¼ mile to a graded road turning right. Turn right (east) on this road and continue for about two miles to the junction with another graded road. Turn right on this road and continue for less than three miles to a boat ramp on Alexander Creek.

Information about the conditions on these forest roads should be obtained from a ranger before setting out.

Juniper Springs and Juniper Creek

Juniper Springs Recreation Area to U.S. 19 (A–B): 7 miles

DIFFICULTY: Easy
SCENERY: Superb
COUNTY: Marion

ACCESS: From Ocala, travel east on S.R. 40 to the Juniper Springs Recreation Area.

TRIP DESCRIPTION: Juniper Springs is said to be one of the clearest streams in Florida. The springhead is enclosed in a rock and concrete wall that provides a large swimming pool. The water flows out of the pool through a flume that powers a waterwheel once used for generating electricity.

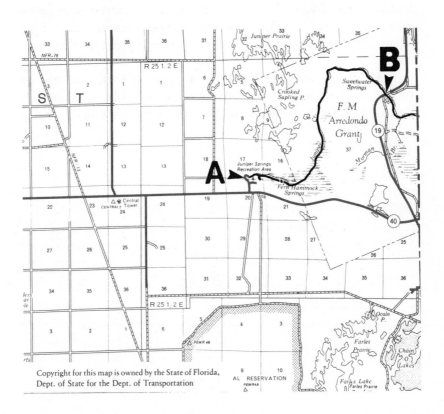

Copyright for this map is owned by the State of Florida,
Dept. of State for the Dept. of Transportation

The first two miles of the stream are very narrow and constricted with palm trees, dense vegetation, and a remarkable population of birds. The national forest has provided a recreation area called Half-Way Landing just before the stream begins to widen. The is not an access point, but simply a place to picnic and relax. There is no public access to Juniper Creek from the launching area to S.R. 19.

After Half-Way Landing, the stream broadens into large grassy areas and divides around hammocks of palms and grass. Alligators, frequently seen in this area, are so accustomed to canoeists that they are not shy and therefore may be dangerous. The open area continues to S.R. 19 where the access is on the southeast side of the bridge. The stream continues for another three miles to Lake George, but there is no access for several miles and the lake is a large body of water.

Canoes can be rented at the Juniper Springs Recreation Area concession stand. Shuttle service from S.R. 19 is included in the price of rental. Private canoes can arrange for a shuttle as well on a space available basis. Most of the year, the heavy concentration of rental canoes on the shuttle makes it time consuming to wait for space for a private craft and most private canoeists prefer to arrange their own shuttle.

TAKE-OUT (B): From the Juniper Springs Recreation Area, travel east on S.R. 40 for four miles, to the intersection with S.R. 19. Turn left (north) on S.R. 19 and continue for four miles to the bridge across Juniper Creek.

Salt Springs and Salt Springs Run

Salt Springs is a large spring whose waters have a high degree of salt content. The pool is about 110 feet in diameter and is roped off as a swimming area. The run down to Lake George is four miles long; there is no access to a take-out, so canoeists must paddle down to the lake and back. The stream is broad and clear, similar to the lower sections of the runs from Juniper and Alexander springs. It is a very remote area and has an abundance of bird life. Pre-Columbian cultural sites are located along the banks of this run and it is said to have exceptional environmental value.

Salt Springs is located within sight of S.R. 19 at the little community of Salt Springs.

Oklawaha River

The Oklawaha River has been the center of one of the most prolonged environmental controversies in Florida. Slated to be the primary vehicle for the Florida Cross State Canal, it has been extensively channelized and developed. The canal project has been abandoned at present, and some sections of the river remain in their original wilderness state.

Beginning in a series of large lakes including Lake Dora, Lake Griffin, and Lake Eustis, the Oklawaha flows over sixty miles in a northern direction to the St. Johns River. Its primary tributary is the Silver River, the outflow from Silver Springs. It also received overflow from Orange Lake through Orange Creek and has a number of smaller feeder streams as well.

The Oklawaha is said to be a very old river geologically and as a result has created a mile-wide valley. It has a sand bottom and its waters tend to be very clear with occasional areas where the tannin from the swamps colors the water in a darker hue. The lower areas have deciduous trees such as tupelo, gums, red maple, sweet bay and some outstanding examples of the bald cypress. When the terrain is higher, upland hardwoods such as oak, magnolia, and beech predominate.

Animal and bird life are abundant with the usual raccoons, skunks, and armadillos present as well as deer, foxes, and otters. Fishing is said to be excellent with catfish, red-breasted bream, shellcrackers, and speckled perch being most sought after.

South of the Moss Bluff Dam, the Oklawaha flows through a series of lakes and alternates between being a defined stream and being scattered and divided among hammocks and islands. North of the Eureka Dam the river is wider and more like a lake. Generally, the best trip for canoeists is the 31 miles between these two points.

Moss Bluff Dam to State Road 40 (A–B): 13 miles

DIFFICULTY: Easy
SCENERY: Fair to Good
COUNTY: Marion

ACCESS: From Ocala, travel east on S.R. 40 thirteen miles to the intersection with S.R. 314 A. Turn right and continue for seven miles to the Moss Bluff Lock and Dam. Access is via a concrete boat ramp on the east side of the river.

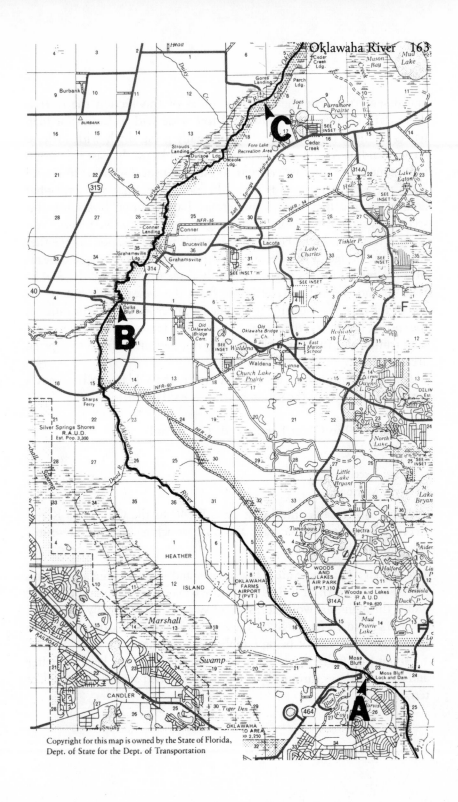

TRIP DESCRIPTION: For the first four miles of this section the river is deep, dark colored, and about 100 feet wide with twenty-foot high banks or dikes on each side. It is virtually a big ditch with little to recommend it. As the trip progresses, the banks on the east side begin to become lower and there is more forestation near the water. In several spots there are large stands of bald cypress trees that are somewhat unique because they are so numerous. Large fishing boats use this section; because it is so long and straight, they can run very fast.

At S.R. 314 (Sharps Ferry), it is possible to put a canoe in on either side of the bridge. The river narrows to about 50 feet wide and beautiful hardwood forests begin. It is only three miles from S.R. 314 to S.R. 40 and the Silver River enters from the west shortly before the end of the trip. It is possible to paddle up Silver River for four miles to the spring, but the current is very swift, there tends to be heavy motorboat traffic, and the concessionaires do not permit traffic in the spring area.

Below the confluence with Silver River, the Oklawaha becomes a clear green color and the sandy bottom is easily seen.

State Road 40 to Gores Landing (B–C): 10 miles

DIFFICULTY: Easy
SCENERY: Excellent
COUNTY: Marion

ACCESS: From Ocala, travel east on S.R. 40 to the Oklawaha River. Access is at a large public park and boat launching area on the southwest side of the bridge.

TRIP DESCRIPTION: There are a few houses and some pastureland during the first mile north of S.R. 40, but the banks soon drop and the river winds through hardwood forests and swamp. Occasionally there will be bluffs up to 15 feet high on the east bank and these often have rope swings and evidence of being established campsites.

About four miles north on this section, small streams began to enter and the river flows through a very heavily wooded area with junglelike terrain.

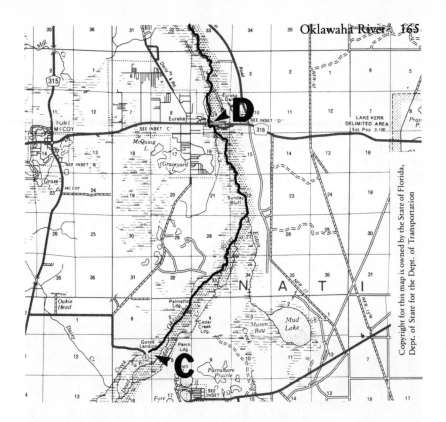

Gores Landing to State Road 316 (C–D): 10 miles

DIFFICULTY: Moderate
SCENERY: Excellent
COUNTY: Marion

ACCESS: From Ocala travel east on S.R. 40 for six miles to the intersection of S.R. 315. Turn left and continue on S.R. 315 for five and one-half miles. Turn right on the first paved road to the right and follow it to Gores Landing. Access is down a paved boat ramp to the river.

TRIP DESCRIPTION: There is a public campground with boat ramp and bathhouse at Gores Landing. The river retains its clear green color until the confluence with Eaton Creek which drains from Mud Lake. Also in this section are Dead River and Cedar Creek where short side trips may be made.

North of the confluence with Eaton Creek there is a very high bluff along the east bank with some houses on top. This appears to be an area that has been used for camping. From this point to Eureka is only two miles.

TAKE-OUT (D): From Fort McCoy, travel east on S.R. 316 for less than four miles to the river. There is a concrete boat ramp on the east side of the river just south of the bridge. A short canal just north of the bridge leads to a store/canoe livery.

Below S.R. 316, the river enters the area that has been flooded by the Eureka Dam. Many canoeists enjoy this section because of the wide variation of bird life that can be observed. It is lake canoeing, however, and can be windy. For the paddler who chooses this section, there is an access eight miles north at Cypress Bayou. It is also possible to paddle an additional ten miles to Orange Springs.

Oklawaha River
Photograph by Elizabeth Carter

Wekiva River and the Rock Springs Run

The Wekiva River in Orange County begins at Wekiwa Springs State Park and flows north for fifteen miles to the St. Johns River. Rock Springs is located seven miles to the northwest, near Apopka, and flows southeast into the Wekiva River about one-half mile below Wekiva Springs. There is no access at Wekiwa Springs State Park so the canoeist must either put in at King's Landing just below Rock Springs and paddle down to the Wekiva, or put in at Wekiva Marina and paddle upstream to Wekiva Springs. Both of these streams are very popular, are located near a large metropolitan area, and are likely to be crowded during the warm months and on weekends. They are beautiful waterways, however, and have maintained a surprising degree of remoteness and freedom from encroachment. The primary distraction is the incredible number of aluminum cans that can be seen through the crystal clear water. The lower portion of the Wekiva River is marred by a collection of squatters' shacks that are up on the islands and swampy hammocks.

As one nears the St. Johns River, the Wekiva becomes very broad and developed. To avoid paddling into a potentially windy and unpleasant experience on the St. Johns, most canoeists prefer to take out about four miles above the confluence at one of several privately owned landings.

Black Water Creek, a tributary of the Wekiva that flows in just above the confluence with the St. Johns is also said to be canoeable. Unfortunately, it has no public access by road.

The terrain on both Wekiva River and Rock Springs Run is a fine example of semitropical Florida wetlands and swamp. Cabbage palm, cypress, and other lowland trees abound, as well as other hardwoods that frequently canopy the waterway. There are a number of campsites on the Rock Springs Run that appear to be well used. After the confluence with the Wekiva River, there are only occasional small sites on unoccupied islands.

King's Landing off State Road 435 to Wekiva Marina (A–B): 8 miles

DIFFICULTY: Easy
SCENERY: Good
COUNTIES: Orange, Seminole

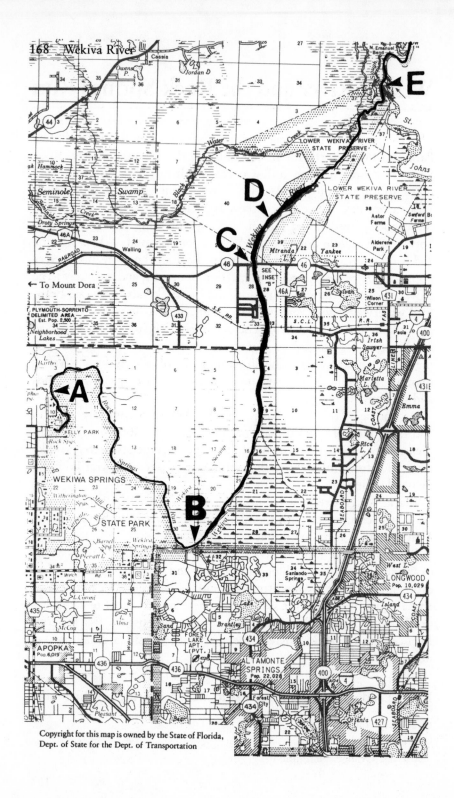

ACCESS: From Apopka, drive north on S.R. 435 for about five miles. Turn right on Kelly Park Road; continue for one-eighth mile and turn left on Camp Joy Road. Continue north for less than a mile to King's Landing. There is a small fee for launching.

TRIP DESCRIPTION: After paddling down a small canal from King's Landing to the Rock Springs Run, one enters a deep channel between lily pads and water reeds. The waterway itself is 30 to 40 feet wide but the navigable channel is only ten to fifteen feet across. There are a few houses on the left (west) bank at the beginning of the trip.

The first four miles of this trail is among the most beautiful examples of lowland hardwoods and clear, green water of any stream in north Florida. Tall trees with slender trunks make a complete canopy over the river in many places. Following this section, the river widens to 50 feet and then up to 100 feet in sections. It is shallower and white sand can be glimpsed between the water weeds on the bottom. There are several campsites along this section.

Some three miles further downstream, the river narrows again to 20 to 30 feet and becomes deeper. The sandy bottom is still in evidence and the canopy of hardwoods resumes. There are also campsites in this area.

At the confluence of the Wekiva River, the canoeists may turn right and paddle up to the entrance to Wekiva Spring. This is the location of a state park, but there are no camping or canoe launching facilities there. There is considerable current in the Wekiva River, but it is only one-half mile to the spring and is worth the effort.

Shortly below the confluence of the Wekiva River with the Rock Springs Run is the Wekiva Marina. This is a privately owned public access facility with canoe rentals, a restaurant, store, and dock. There is also a bridge across the river at this point that does not have a road connected to it (1984).

Wekiva Marina to State Road 46 (B–C): 10 miles

DIFFICULTY: Easy
SCENERY: Good
COUNTIES: Seminole, Orange

ACCESS: From Apopka, travel north on S.R. 435 for less than three miles. Turn right on Welch Road and continue to Wekiwa Springs State Park. Continue one mile east on the Wekiwa Springs State Park

Road to a dirt road that turns north, drive about one-quarter mile to the Wekiva Springs Marina.

TRIP DESCRIPTION: After leaving the marina, the river turns north and fish camp cottages begin to appear on the banks and most of the small islands in the river. The river varies from 50 to 150 feet wide, dividing around the islands. An occasional campsite can be found on unoccupied islands. The Little Wekiva River enters from the right three miles downstream. A railroad trestle is another five miles downstream.

The river widens dramatically just below the trestle to over three hundred feet and resembles a small lake of grass and reeds. In this area, a canal on the left bank leads to a tourist attraction called Wekiva Falls. This facility has canoe rentals, camping, and a small riverboat that tours up the Wekiva for a mile or so. This shallow, grassy area continues to S.R. 46.

State Road 46 to Katie's Landing or the St. Johns River (C–D, E): 1–6 miles

DISTANCE: 1–6 miles
DIFFICULTY: Easy
SCENERY: Good
COUNTIES: Seminole, Lake, Volusia

ACCESS: From Mount Dora, travel east on S.R. 46 for about 12 miles. The access is on the northeast side of the bridge.

TRIP DESCRIPTION: One mile below S.R. 46, the Wekiva narrows again, becomes deeper, and the current resumes. In places, the hardwood almost canopy the river. Wekiva Park Drive runs beside the river on the east bank for about one mile. There are two privately owned boat launch areas off this road, Katie's Wekiva River Landing and Wekiva Haven. Unless one plans to paddle down to and across the St. Johns River, it is best to choose one of these spots to take out.

From the end of Wekiva Park Drive, there are four miles of dense swamp through the Lower Wekiva River State Preserve. The river widens again before reaching the St. Johns, and a tributary, Black Water Creek enters from the west.

TAKE-OUT (D): After crossing the Wekiva River going east on S.R. 46, turn left on the first road beside the river; this is Wekiva Park Drive. If taking out on the St. Johns (E), the access is off High Banks Road in Volusia County.

St. Marys River

The St. Marys River is the border between the states of Georgia and Florida east of the Okefenokee Swamp in Georgia. The North Prong of the St. Marys flows out of the edges of the Okefenokee Swamp, while the Middle Prong begins on the east side of Buckhead Swamp in the Big Gum Swamp in the Osceola National Forest. The two streams join shortly below S.R. 120 in extreme north Florida to form the St. Marys River which flows to the Atlantic Ocean near Fernandina Beach.

Although it is over 125 miles long, it is one of Florida's lesser known waterways. For its first 40 miles, the St. Marys forms a horseshoe, flowing due south for 10 miles, then due east for 12 miles, then due north again. Florida S.R. 2 crosses the St. Marys twice, defining the upper limits of the horseshoe. Above S.R. 2, the river continues in its northern course for some 33 miles before heading east to the Atlantic. This wide, meandering curve, combined with the many long bends in the river, can lead to directional confusion for the canoeist who is not aware of the river's orientation.

The upper reaches of the St. Marys, the North and Middle prongs, are narrow, twisting streams with good current and beautiful cypress and tupelo trees. After confluence, the river becomes wider and is characterized by bluffs, swamps, and snow-white sandbars. It is an excellent touring river since development along the banks is scattered and infrequent and campsites are plentiful. Trees indigenous to north Florida are found along the St. Marys including stands of cypress and yellow pine, gum, magnolia, maple, holly, poplar, willow, and river birch. Wildlife in this area includes deer, otter, beaver, raccoon, and alligator. The Middle Prong is said to provide a habitat for bear, panther, bobcat, and the red-cockaded woodpecker.

Middle Prong

State Road 250 to State Road 127 (A1–B1): 10 miles

DIFFICULTY: Moderate
SCENERY: Excellent
COUNTY: Baker

ACCESS: From Glen St. Mary, travel north on S.R. 125 to the junction

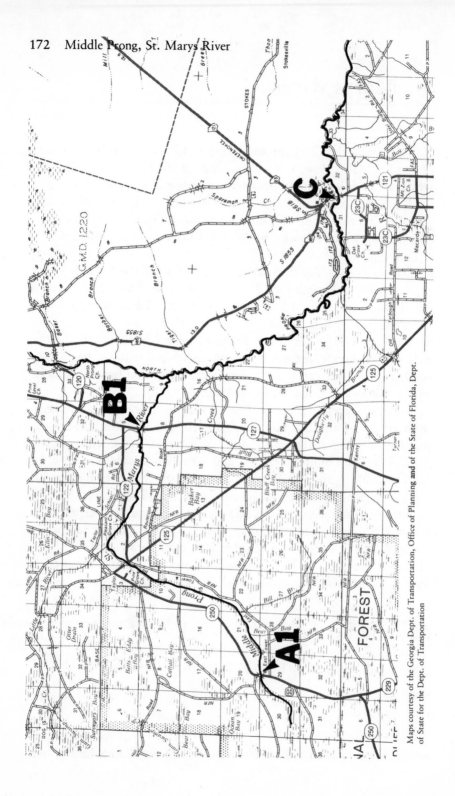

Maps courtesy of the Georgia Dept. of Transportation, Office of Planning and of the State of Florida, Dept. of State for the Dept. of Transportation

with S.R. 250. Turn left (south) and continue for 4.5 miles to the river. The access is on the southeast side of the bridge in a large pond.

TRIP DESCRIPTION: This section starts in a pond and the stream exits from the northeast end. Although this is a very swampy area, the creek maintains a clearly defined current. There are many downed trees and other obstructions that make this a moderately strenuous trip. There are stands of willow trees above and below the S.R. 125 bridge and there is access to the stream on the northwest side of the bridge. Just a mile further down, at S.R. 122, there is a better access. As one progresses downstream, the terrain changes from lowlands and swampy areas to higher banks and upland pine forests. This section would not be canoeable in very dry weather.

State Road 127 to Junction with the North Prong (B1–C): 2 miles

DIFFICULTY: Easy
SCENERY: Good
COUNTY: Baker

ACCESS: From Glen St. Mary, travel north on S.R. 125 to the junction with S.R. 127. Turn right (north) and continue just over four miles to the Middle Prong of the St. Marys River. Access is on the northwest side of the bridge.

TRIP DESCRIPTION: This stream continues with high banks and a good current down to its confluence with the North Prong of the St. Marys River. The next access is on the St. Marys at S.R. 121, a distance of about nine miles.

North Prong

State Road 2 to State Road 120 (A–B): 5 miles

DIFFICULTY: Moderate
SCENERY: Excellent
COUNTY: Baker

ACCESS: From Glen St. Mary, travel north on S.R. 125 for seven miles to the junction with S.R. 127. Turn right (north) on S.R. 127 and

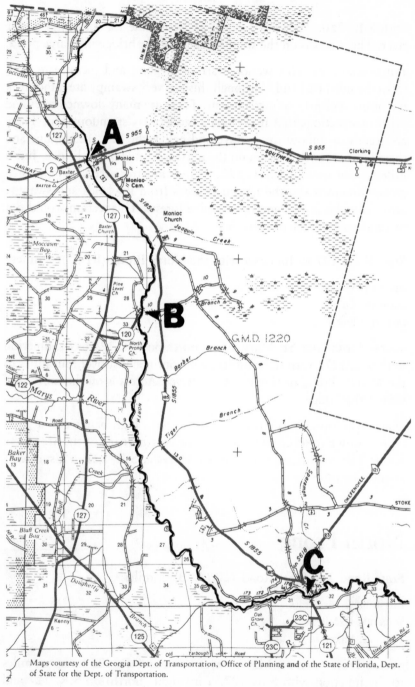

Maps courtesy of the Georgia Dept. of Transportation, Office of Planning and of the State of Florida, Dept.
of State for the Dept. of Transportation.

continue for ten miles to the intersection with S.R. 2. Turn right (east) and continue less than one mile to the river. Access is on the southeast side of the bridge.

TRIP DESCRIPTION: This upper section of the North Prong is narrow with high banks and a good current. Cypress and tupelo trees grow in the stream resulting in obstacles that require skill in maneuvering. The water is a dark tannin color and the white sand bottom can be glimpsed in the shallows. The banks rise after the first two miles and tend to be steep and inaccessible. Just north of the S.R. 120 bridge one begins to encounter small islands in the river and there is a house on the west bank. Just before reaching the bridge there is a larger island with swift channels on either side. This section may be difficult in low water.

State Road 120 to State Road 121 (B–C): 12 miles

DIFFICULTY: Moderate to Easy
SCENERY: Excellent
COUNTY: Baker

ACCESS: From Glen St. Mary, travel north on S.R. 125 for seven miles to the junction with S.R. 127. Turn right (north) on S.R. 127 and continue until it crosses the Middle Prong of the St. Marys. Continue for less than two miles to the intersection with S.R. 120 on the right. Turn right and drive about one mile to the river. Access is down a steep bank on the northwest side of the bridge. This is a difficult access that requires carrying canoes and gear for about 50 yards.

TRIP DESCRIPTION: This section continues with high banks, small islands, and a good current to the confluence with the Middle Prong two miles south. When the two streams meet, the river becomes much wider and shallower with gentle curves and large sandbars. The banks continue to remain high with palmetto and pine forests on top. The river continues in a southern direction for the next eight miles. About two miles above S.R. 121, it turns to the east. There is a row of houses along the south bank one mile above S.R. 121.

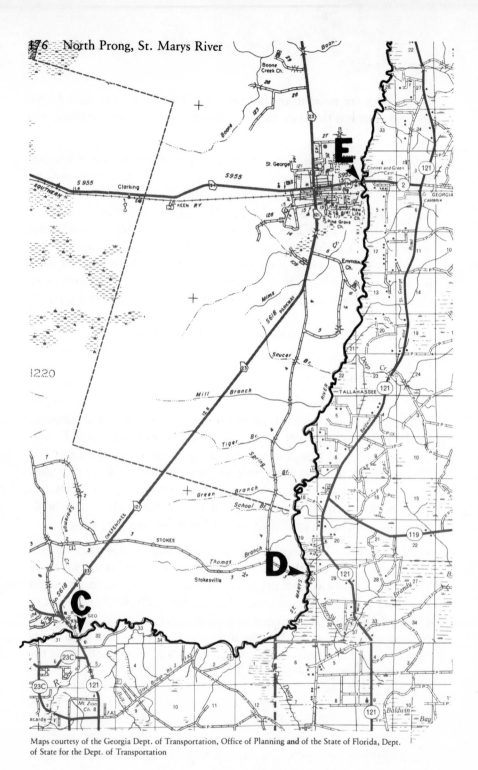

Maps courtesy of the Georgia Dept. of Transportation, Office of Planning and of the State of Florida, Dept. of State for the Dept. of Transportation

State Road 121 to Stokes Bridge (C–D): 9 miles

DIFFICULTY: Easy
SCENERY: Good
COUNTIES: Baker, Nassau

ACCESS: From Macclenny, travel north on S.R. 121 to the river. Access is down a dirt track on the northwest side of the bridge.

TRIP DESCRIPTION: The St. Marys is 50 to 75 feet wide at this access with banks 15 feet high. The current is slow but helpful and in low water downed trees may cause obstructions in the waterway. There is evidence of frequent access to the river on the Florida side for the first few miles, but no houses or public access areas. The river has many twisting turns for the first three miles, then straightens out for two miles. In this straight area, the banks are high and steep. A house is on the Florida side midway down the straight section—at its end is a primitive boat ramp, sandbar, and camping area. This is a good camp-site but may be crowded. After passing this area, the river begins to wind again and there are a number of houses along the bank on the Florida side. About two miles below the houses, the road to Stokes-ville, Georgia, crosses the river.

Stokes Bridge to State Road 2 (D–E): 12 miles

DIFFICULTY: Easy
SCENERY: Excellent
COUNTIES: Baker, Nassau

ACCESS: From Macclenny, travel east on U.S. 90 for just under five miles to the junction with the eastern section of S.R. 121. Turn left (north) on S.R. 121 and continue for less than two miles to the inter-section with a graded road. Turn left (west) and continue for about one-half mile to the river. This is the road that leads to Stokesville, Georgia.

TRIP DESCRIPTION: There are several large sandbars at this access and it is a popular spot for swimming and camping. The river continues its twisting nature for another mile, then begins a three or four mile straight section. There are numerous large, high sandbanks in the twist-ing sections that make good campsites. This variation of twisting stream interspersed with long straight sections continues to the S.R. 2

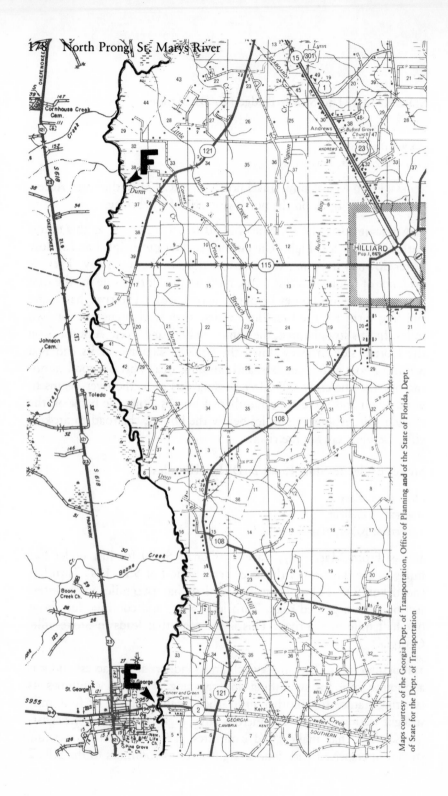

Maps courtesy of the Georgia Dept. of Transportation, Office of Planning and of the State of Florida, Dept. of State for the Dept. of Transportation

bridge. There is limited access to the river for five miles of this section and it is suitably remote and very beautiful. Just above the S.R. 2 bridge are numerous houses on the Georgia side and the sandbanks are obviously accessible by road and are popular for swimming.

State Road 2 to Thompkins Landing (E–F): 17 miles

DIFFICULTY: Easy
SCENERY: Good
COUNTY: Nassau

ACCESS: From Macclenny, travel east on U.S. 90 for just over five miles to the junction with the eastern section of S.R. 121. Turn left (north) and continue to the intersection with S.R. 2. Turn left (west) and continue to the river. Access is on the northwest side of the bridge.

TRIP DESCRIPTION: The river continues to alternate between long stretches with high banks interspersed with wide bends and sandbars. This is a very remote section with little access to the river. Campsites are scattered as the sandbars are not large and the banks are six to seven feet high. About two miles north of S.R. 2, there is an access at Red Bluff on the Florida side. Six miles south of the Thompkins Landing access, pieces of pottery are scattered along and embedded into the banks on the Georgia side. Just north of this spot are the remains of an old bridge.

Thompkins Landing to U.S. 1 (F–G): 11 miles

DIFFICULTY: Easy
SCENERY: Good
COUNTY: Nassau

ACCESS: From Hilliard, travel five miles west on S.R. 115 to the junction with S.R. 121. Turn right (north) and continue for just under two miles until the small bridge across Dunn Creek is reached. Continue for another one-half mile to the first graded road to the left (west). Turn left and continue to the river—this is Thompkins Landing road.

TRIP DESCRIPTION: This is the final section of the St. Marys River that is considered best for canoeing. A concrete boat ramp is at Thompkins Landing as well as a flat, grassy area and some generous sandbars. This

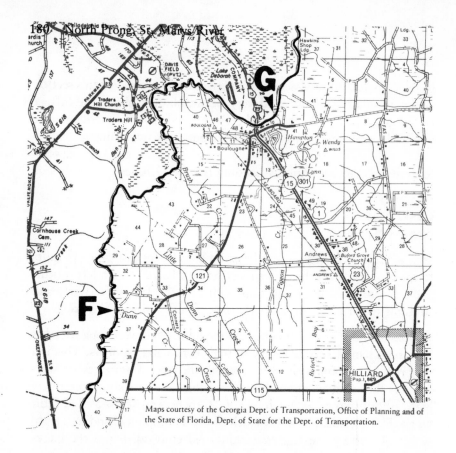

Maps courtesy of the Georgia Dept. of Transportation, Office of Planning and of the State of Florida, Dept. of State for the Dept. of Transportation.

is a popular camping and swimming spot. There are a number of campsites on the right bank for the next mile as well.

The river continues to have 8- to 10-foot banks with alternating straight stretches and wide curves. About two miles north of Thompkins Landing there is a fishing camp on the Georgia side—just north of that a private landing. As one progresses downriver, an occasional short stretch of swampy woods can be seen and there are some stands of tall pines on the higher ground. Some small sloughs with lily pads and marsh grass also begin to appear.

Seven miles from Thompkins Landing, Traders Hill is reached on the Georgia side. A boat ramp, picnic tables, restrooms, and campsites are at the end of a paved road that turns off Georgia S.R. 121 only a few miles south of Folkston. This is a historical spot, having once been the county seat of Charlton County, Georgia. It is the point where riverboats came up the St. Marys to deliver supplies to the area. Some of the wooden pilings from the many docks can still be seen.

Pickney Landing is two miles farther downstream, also on the Georgia side of the river. The river begins to widen at Traders Hill and the Sloughs and evidence of saltwater infiltration are more evident. The Seaboard Railroad trestle crosses the river just one mile before U.S. 1; since this is a very active track, the sound of trains is almost constant as one approaches and leaves the trestle. There is a very poor access on the northwest side of U.S. 1, but it is less than a mile farther to a public boat ramp on the Florida side.

TAKE-OUT (G): From Hilliard, travel north on U.S. 301 for four miles. Just before reaching the St. Marys River, a paved road intersects U.S. 1. Turn right (east) and continue for less than one mile to the first graded road turning left; turn left and continue to a boat ramp on the river.

Although the St. Marys continues for another 47 miles to the Atlantic Ocean from U.S. 1, it is an increasingly wide and tidal river that is popular with very large boats. Canoeists who choose to paddle on to the Atlantic should do so with caution.

North Prong of St. Marys River

Photograph by John Pearce

Black Creek

In an area dominated by the massive St. Johns River with its huge inlets and lakes, Black Creek still provides the type of wilderness canoeing that characterizes north Florida. Flowing north into the St. Johns, Black Creek drains out of a sandy ridge of arid pine lands and scrub oak forests into a cool ravine bordered by a canopy of hardwoods. Like the many other "Black" creeks, rivers, and waters in north Florida, it is named for the darkly stained tannin water that results from the acid produced by the vegetation along its banks and on the banks of the rivulets and streams that feed it.

Black Creek flows for some twenty miles from S.R. 16 near Penney Farms, to the St. Johns. Only the first fourteen miles is considered of interest to the canoeist, however, since the final six miles is extremely broad, tidal, and used extensively by large motorized craft.

State Road 16 to State Road 218 (A–B): 7 miles

DIFFICULTY: Moderate
SCENERY: Excellent
COUNTY: Clay

ACCESS: From Penney Farms, travel west on S.R. 16 to the bridge across Black Creek. Access is down a dirt track on the southeast side of the bridge.

TRIP DESCRIPTION: Since Black Creek is very sensitive to local rainfall, it is essential to check the water gauge under the S.R. 16 bridge. Two to four feet is the optimal level, with water lower than two feet resulting in pull-overs and water above four feet putting the canoeist in the trees.

At the put-in, the creek is twenty-five to thirty feet wide with white sandbanks up to ten feet high. Hardwoods, willows, and scrub oak are prevalent. There is a good current and the water is a clear tea color with the white sand bottom in evidence. The stream twists and turns with numerous logs and submerged stumps to surprise the unwary. About one mile downstream, a rock ledge across the creek makes an interesting rapid. There is a treehouse perched high on the bank on the west side, followed by a section of high rock banks covered with fern and lichen. Occasionally there will be a high sand bluff. Both banks of the river have posted signs making camping questionable.

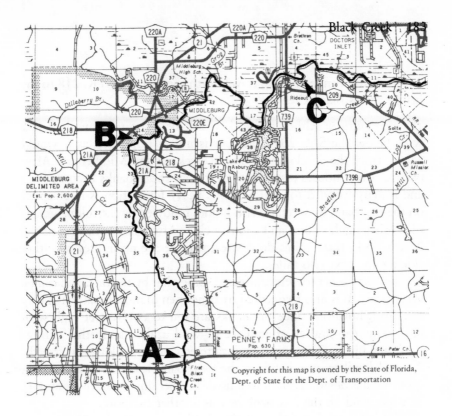

For the first three miles the stream alternates these high banks with curves and a corridor of hardwoods. During the fourth mile, houses and mobile homes begin to appear at intervals on the west bank and the stream flows past the pilings of an old bridge. In the fifth mile, more elaborate houses appear, set well back from the river. Finally, in the two miles above the S.R. 218 bridge, the west bank becomes much more developed with very large motorboats tied up to private docks or housed in boat houses. The east bank of the river is undeveloped until just before the bridge. In this last two miles the stream has become much broader and slower and small sloughs with lily pads are seen. For the dedicated wilderness canoeist, this first section of Black Creek provides a pleasant canoeing experience.

State Road 218 to State Road 209 (B–C): 7 miles

DIFFICULTY: Moderate
SCENERY: Good
COUNTY: Clay

ACCESS: From Penney Farms, travel north then west on S.R. 218 to the bridge across Black Creek.

TRIP DESCRIPTION: Although Black Creek becomes two hundred feet wide below the S.R. 209 bridge, it is not as populated as it would appear from the development on the creek around Middleburg. After passing a few houses just below the bridge, both banks become high and heavily wooded for a time. This heavy forestation is interrupted on the east bank by several lavish homes followed by the rolling greens of a private golf course and country club. After the confluence of the North Fork, three miles downstream, there are no houses on either side for the next two miles.

This section is very wide, affected somewhat by the tide, and can be very windy. It is also frequented by fishermen in motorboats. It is very beautiful, however, since the banks are ten to twelve feet high with large oak trees and an abundance of wild azaleas and other spring-flowering plants. There are a few scattered campsites along this stretch. A small sandbar on a bend on the west bank leads up to a camping spot that has obviously been well used. Further down, another glimmer of white sand on the east bank reveals another campsite.

Within two miles of the S.R. 209 bridge, intensive development on the east bank begins again. The west bank is still wild until the bridge is sighted. At the S.R. 209 bridge the creek is very wide and is beginning to be populated with large boats.

Although the remainder of the creek has some lovely spots, it is a chore for the canoeist to combat wind, tide, and the wake from motorized craft to reach the St. Johns.

TAKE-OUT (C): From Penney Farms, travel north on S.R. 218 to the junction with S.R. 739. Continue north on S.R. 739 for three miles to the intersection with S.R. 209. Turn right on S.R. 209 and continue for less than one mile to Old Ferry Road. Turn left on Old Ferry Road and continue to a boat launch area on the creek.

Canoe Liveries and Outfitters

AAA Canoe Rental
Route 2, Box 578
Cantonment, Florida 32533
(904) 587-2366
Joe and Dee Riley
Perdido/Styx Rivers

Adventures Unlimited
P.O. Box 40
Bagdad, Florida 32530
(904) 623-6197
Jack and Esther Sanborn
Mike and Linda Sanborn
Coldwater, Blackwater,
Juniper Rivers

Adventures Unlimited
Perdido River
Route 4, Box 68
Cantonment, Florida 32533
(904) 968-5529
David and Linda Venn
Perdido River

Alexander Springs Concession
P.O. Box 112
Astor, Florida 32002
(904) 759-2365
Roger Williams
Alexander Springs Creek

Bob's Canoes
Route 8, Box 34
Milton, Florida 32570
(904) 623-5457
L.L. and Marie Plowman
Coldwater, Blackwater,
Sweetwater, Juniper
Rivers

Canoe Outpost - Nobelton
P.O. Box 188, S.R. 476
Nobelton, Florida 33554
(904) 696-4343
George and Debby Blust
South Withlacoochee

Canoe Outpost - Suwannee
Route 1, Box 346
Live Oak, Florida 32060
(904) 842-2192
Suwannee, Alapaha,
Withlacoochee North
Rivers

Down River Canoe Trips, Inc.
P.O. Box 837
Tallahassee, Florida 32302
(904) 222-5546
Elizabeth Carter
Guided trips on north
Florida rivers

Katie's Wekiva River Landing
Route 1, Box 184
Sanford, Florida 32771
(305) 322-4470
Katie Moncrief
Wekiva, Rock Springs Run,
St. Johns Rivers

Oklawaha Canoe Outpost
Route 1, Box 1462
Fort McCoy, Florida 32637
(904) 236-4606
Robert and Bonnie Morrissey
Oklawaha River

Santa Fe Canoe Outpost
Box 592
High Springs, Florida 32643
(904) 454-2050
Ulrich and Irene Gonitzke
Santa Fe, Ichetucknee Rivers

The Canoe Shop
1115-B West Orange Avenue
Tallahassee, Florida 32310
(904) 576-5335
Sam Lamar
250 mile radius of Tallahassee

The Canoe Livery
Route 2, Box 222C
Newton, Alabama 36352
(205) 299-3888
Jim Bloxsom and Butch Grafton
Choctawhatchee River

Canoe Outfitters
P.O. Box 2192
Valdosta, Georgia 31601
(912) 247-0408
Alapaha, Suwannee,
Withlacoochee North
Rivers

This list was compiled from the Fifth Edition (1983) of the *Canoe Liveries and Outfitters Directory.* For information about liveries not included, check the Yellow Pages of the telephone book for towns near the rivers you wish to canoe.

Index

Italic page numbers indicate maps.

Other Menasha Ridge Press Books

A Hiking Guide to the Trails of Florida, Elizabeth F. Carter

The Squirt Book: The Manual of Squirt Kayaking Technique, James E. Snyder, illustrated by W. Nealy

Chattooga River Flip Map (Section IV), Ron Rathnow

Nantahala River Flip Map, Ron Rathnow

New River Flip Map, Ron Rathnow

Ocoee River Flip Map, Ron Rathnow

Youghiogheny River Flip Map, Ron Rathnow

Kayak: The Animated Manual of Intermediate and Advanced White-water Technique, William Nealy

Kayaks to Hell, William Nealy

Whitewater Home Companion, Southeastern Rivers, Volume I, William Nealy

Whitewater Home Companion, Southeastern Rivers, Volume II, William Nealy

Whitewater Tales of Terror, William Nealy

Carolina Whitewater: A Canoeist's Guide to the Western Carolinas, Bob Benner

A Paddler's Guide to Eastern North Carolina, Bob Benner and Tom McCloud

Wildwater West Virginia, Volume I, The Northern Streams, Paul Davidson, Ward Eister, and Dirk Davidson

Wildwater West Virginia, Volume II, The Southern Streams, Paul Davidson, Ward Eister, and Dirk Davidson

Diver's Guide to Underwater America, Kate Kelley and John Shobe

Shipwrecks: Diving the Graveyard of the Atlantic, Roderick M. Farb

Boatbuilder's Manual, Charles Walbridge, editor

Smoky Mountains Trout Fishing Guide, Don Kirk

Fishing the Great Lakes of the South: An Angler's Guide to the TVA System, Don and Joann Kirk

A Fishing Guide to Kentucky's Major Lakes, Arthur B. Lander, Jr.

A Guide to the Backpacking and Day-Hiking Trails of Kentucky, Arthur B. Lander, Jr.

A Canoeing and Kayaking Guide to the Streams of Florida, Volume I, North Central Peninsula and Panhandle, Elizabeth F. Carter and John L. Pearce

A Canoeing and Kayaking Guide to the Streams of Florida, Volume II, Central and South Peninsula, Lou Glaros and Doug Sphar